Humanized Input

OTHER BOOKS BY TOM GILB

1973   *Reliable EDP Application Design (Studentlitteratur)*

1974   *Controlling the Computer (Studentlitteratur)*

1976   *Data Engineering (Studentlitteratur)*

1976   *Software Metrics (Studentlitteratur/Winthrop)*

OTHER BOOKS BY GERALD M. WEINBERG

1961   *Computer Programming Fundamentals (with H. D. Leeds) (McGraw-Hill)*

1966   *PL/I Programming Primer (McGraw-Hill)*

1970   *Computer Programming Fundamentals, Based on the IBM System/360 (with H. D. Leeds) (McGraw-Hill)*

1970   *PL/I Programming--A Manual of Style (McGraw-Hill)*

1971   *The Psychology of Computer Programming (Van Nostrand-Reinhold)*

1973   *Structured Programming in PL/C: An Abecedarian (with Norie F. Yasukawa and Robert Marcus) (John Wiley & Sons)*

1975   *An Introduction to General Systems Thinking (Wiley Interscience)*

1975   *Structured Programming Film Series (with Dennis Geller and Tom Plum) (Edutronics)*

1976   *High Level COBOL Programming (with Steve Wright, Dick Kauffman, and Marty Goetz) (Winthrop)*

WINTHROP COMPUTER SYSTEMS SERIES
Gerald M. Weinberg, editor

Published:

Conway and Gries, AN INTRODUCTION TO PROGRAMMING:
A STRUCTURED APPROACH USING PL/I AND PL/C-7, 2nd ed.

Conway and Gries, PRIMER ON STRUCTURED PROGRAMMING
USING PL/I, PL/C, AND PL/CT

Conway, Gries, and Zimmerman, A PRIMER ON PASCAL

Geller and Freedman, STRUCTURED PROGRAMMING IN APL

Gilb, SOFTWARE METRICS

Gilb and Weinberg, HUMANIZED INPUT: TECHNIQUES FOR
RELIABLE KEYED INPUT

To be published:

Conway, Gries, and Wortman, INTRODUCTION TO STRUCT-
URED PROGRAMMING USING PL/I AND SP/K

Eckhouse and Spier, GUIDE TO PROGRAMMING

Finkenaur, COBOL FOR STUDENTS: A PROGRAMMING PRIMER

Geller, STRUCTURED PROGRAMMING IN FORTRAN

Greenfield, THE ARCHITECTURE OF MICROCOMPUTERS

Topping, SIMULA PROGRAMMING

Weinberg, Goetz, Wright, and Kauffman, HIGH LEVEL
COBOL PROGRAMMING

Wilcox, INTRODUCTION TO COMPILER CONSTRUCTION

Humanized Input

Techniques for Reliable Keyed Input

Tom Gilb

Gerald M. Weinberg

Winthrop Publishers, Inc.
Cambridge, Massachusetts

188645

Library of Congress Cataloging in Publication Data

Gilb, Tom.
    Humanized input.

    (Winthrop computer systems series)
    1. Input design, Computer. I. Weinberg,
Gerald M., joint author. II. Title.
QA76.9.I55G54   001.6'442   76-26562
ISBN 0-87626-345-7

Tom Gilb, Iver Holters Vei 2, N-141- Kolbotn, Norway
Telephone: (472) - 80 16 97

Gerald M. Weinberg, Ethnotech, Inc., Lincoln, Nebraska

To the thousands of keypunch "girls,"
who have saved so many awful designs
by the tips of their fingers,
we offer this work.

Contents

Preface

This book of mine has little need of preface,
for indeed it is "all preface" from beginning to end.

> --D'Arcy Wentworth Thompson
> *On Growth and Form*

In the world of systems design, programs and data are the scissor blades working together to form the broader class--software. Lacking either blade, computers couldn't cut through problems--yet for many people, "software" is synonymous with "programs."

Program design is an integral part of the training of the average systems analyst, designer, or programmer. In the course of that training, the instructors will acknowledge the theoretical significance of data, but will convey little sense of how to design it.

Certainly we still have much to learn about program design, but data design has barely been discovered. A few people have ideas about designing data; even fewer have set their ideas on paper. Therefore, almost any attempt to collect and codify the scattered bits of data design thinking should pay top dividends.

A HANDBOOK

We decided that the most valuable form of presenting what we and others had learned about data design
was a *handbook*. A handbook, if successful, will be
kept on the desk of the designer and consulted with
profit each time a fresh design problem presents itself. At the very least, a handbook should make the
designer aware of new possibilities--ones that were
never used because they were never considered.

WHY INPUT?

The volume at hand represents the first of several contemplated volumes on data design. Why start
with input? For one thing, it's the *beginning* of data
as data, the birth of computerized information. Badly
born data poison the bloodstream of any system, making
other design effort more like emergency care than
health planning.

Secondly, most of today's meager data design literature concentrates on other issues--areas such as
"data structure" and "data base." If we are unable to
cope with growing input problems, new writings in
these glamourous areas will be futile. Someone has to
do the mundane work, so why not us?

Thirdly, we believe that computers exist for
people, not the reverse. Quite often, the people/
computer interface is unpleasant for the senior
partner. Life was hard enough before computers appeared, yet life should be pleasant--for people, if not
for computers.

Finally, when life *isn't* pleasant for people,
those people will make life unpleasant for computers,
one way or another, but usually through input. So
whether you're devoted to people or computers, the
conclusion is the same--if input design fails, the
system fails.

WHY KEYED?

Not all computer input originates in keystrokes,

but in a commercial environment, 99% of it does. Other input sources include

> direct readout from measuring devices
>
> digitizers, as for input of map or contour information
>
> drawings made with a light pen or similar device
>
> voice recognizers

These inputs are ultimately digitized for computer use, but not by the depression of keys with the fingers. It's not by accident that the basic units of information in computers are called *digits*, from the Latin *digitus*, or the English *digit*, meaning a finger. (Sometimes it also means a toe, so we won't automatically rule out toe-driven devices.)

Most computing starts with someone pressing a key with a finger, or otherwise creating a digit. Sometimes the digits are written by hand, so no actual key is pressed. In a few cases, spoken digits can now be recognized. Much of what we have to say about keyed input will apply to those situations as well. Another way of putting it is that we are dealing with "alphanumeric" input, or "character" input--yet both these choices are somewhat inexact, like "keyed."

No doubt the future of computing will see much more use of "exotic" input forms that will not fall under our somewhat narrowed scope. Fortunately, readers interested in these areas have an excellent source in Jim Martin's book, *Design of Man-Computer Dialogues*, with the further advantage that Martin's book also considers *outputs*. On the whole, there is very little overlap between our book and Martin's. What he does well, we felt no need to do over. We only hope to do our things as well as he does.

WHY RELIABLE?

One of the lessons of this book is that *design is multidimensional*. Indeed, many readers will already be familiar with Gilb's work on design, and thus expect to hear about the balancing of objectives, etc., etc. They may also be familiar with Gilb's "Laws of Unreliability" (1975), in which case they won't be surprised by the emphasis in the title--though they still may not understand it. But Weinberg, too, has laws, and one of them concerns the *special* role of reliability in design. Weinberg thinks it comes before Gilb's nine laws, so he calls it the "Zeroth Law of Unreliability":

> IF A SYSTEM DOESN'T HAVE TO BE RELIABLE,
> IT CAN MEET ANY OTHER OBJECTIVE.

In other words, out of all possible objectives, *reliability* stands alone. We can always make a system faster, smaller, more portable, cheaper, or anything else--*if it doesn't have to do what it was specified to do*.

The only reason Gilb didn't make that one of his laws of unreliability is that he thought it was obvious. Weinberg, being less bright, but older, knew people who didn't understand the zeroth law--people who designed wonderful systems with only one flaw: They didn't work.

Of course, many systems--probably most systems-- "work" in one fashion or another. They're not *totally* unreliable, and sometimes, or even frequently, they do the right thing and avoid the wrong thing. Indeed, no system is *absolutely* reliable, or, as Gilb's Eighth Law states:

> ALL REAL PROGRAMS CONTAIN ERRORS UNTIL PROVED OTHERWISE--
> WHICH IS IMPOSSIBLE.

To which Weinberg would add (Gilb thinking it obvious):

> ALL REAL DATA COLLECTIONS CONTAIN ERRORS UNTIL PROVED
> OTHERWISE--WHICH IS LIKEWISE IMPOSSIBLE.

So, reliability is a relative thing, and Weinberg's Zeroth Law could be restated:

> THE LESS RELIABLE A SYSTEM HAS TO BE, THE MORE EASILY
> IT CAN MEET ANY OTHER OBJECTIVE.

Or, as one engineer put it:

IF YOU DON'T HAVE TO MEET THE SPECIFICATIONS,
YOU CAN BUILD A MASTERPIECE.

WHY DATA RELIABILITY?

But aren't *program* bugs much more of a problem
than data errors? Shouldn't we concentrate on program
reliability, instead? C. A. R. Hoare (1975) has given
a strong description of why data reliability is so
important, by contrasting data reliability with program reliability--which we all know is important.
Hoare gives these four points of contrast:

> *(1) Programs expressed in a suitable high level
> language can be analysed rigorously by a compiler
> so that a running program is known to be meaning-
> ful, even if it does not do what the programmer
> wanted. Input data is nothing but an unstruct-
> ured stream of characters, cards, or bits; it may
> be meaningless, and even if meaningful, the in-
> formation conveyed may be false.*

> *(2) If a program behaves incorrectly on a par-
> ticular run, this does not affect other programs,
> or even subsequent runs of the same program.
> However, if a bug is introduced on one run into a
> data base, it remains there, and can actually
> propogate itself as later correct programs oper-
> ate on the data.*

> *(3) If the hardware fails in the middle of a run
> of a program, it can safely be run again from the
> beginning, but the same fault in the midst of
> updating a data base may leave it in a partially
> or wholly unusable condition.*

> *(4) From bitter experience, users can learn to
> avoid the bugs in unreliable software. But as
> soon as bugs appear in a data bank, its users
> lose confidence, and will withdraw their data for
> private keeping. Now they no longer have any
> motive to keep their banked data up-to-date. A
> run on a data bank is as catastrophic as a run on
> an ordinary bank which deals merely in money.*

Not all of Hoare's points deal directly with *input* reliability, but all are at least indirectly related to the problem at hand. To Hoare's points we might add a fifth:

> *(5)   When a data error enters a system, it is less likely than a program error to cause something noticeable to happen.   These hidden "mutations" will thus tend to accumulate in the system as a "genetic load"--a slower but more certain destruction of the system than a dramatic "run on the data bank."   Weinberg (1970) has given a fuller description of this process.*

When we consider the *interaction* of program and data, a sixth point becomes evident:

> *(6)   Program errors often create data errors which are then stored in the data bank, so unreliable programming tends to produce unreliable data.   Data errors, on the other hand, tend to reveal things about the structure of the program, as they lead the program through previously untrodden paths.   Much of the early improvement of new systems stems from unanticipated interaction with incorrect data.   Thus, data errors help programming, but programming errors complicate the data situation.*

Finally, we should add an observation about the social and economic environment of data and programs:

> *(7)   Programming is more or less understood to be a highly-skilled, well-paid profession, so we can expect improvement in programming as the profession matures.   So far, data entry is considered to be a low-skilled, poorly-paid form of low-esteem labor.   Under these conditions, we can hardly hope for improvement in the intrinsic quality of input data--but we can certainly anticipate a worsening as systems grow more complex.*

In short, if you think things are bad now, just wait a few years and you'll be yearning for the "good old days"--unless, of course, we succeed in teaching the lessons of this book.

Acknowledgments

Hundreds of people contribute to a handbook such as this, yet most of them cannot be recognized explicitly for their contribution. To the unnamed students, clients, and colleagues who have given so freely of so many ideas and so much time, we give the heartiest possible thanks. To our families and friends, who must put up with the many pains and few joys of authorship, we wish also to say thank you--however inadequate those words may be.

Special thanks are due to Mike Meehan of Winthrop Publishers, who encouraged and abetted this difficult transoceanic cross-cultural collaboration, and also to the entire staff of Winthrop who labored to produce the book.

The readers may wish to add to our own profuse thanks to Mary Hutchinson, without whose firm editorial hand this book would have been ten times more difficult to read and ten times less useful. If there are errors remaining (as we know there must be) it is only because of the great number in the input, not because of any inadequacy of Mary's verification procedures.

Most authors end this section with an acknowledgement of the typist or typesetter whose keystrokes made the whole thing possible, but we cannot do so. The senior author believes it would be inappropriate to thank the junior author who--out of moral conviction and a desire for the empathetic experience--typed virtually the entire book as you now read it. The reader, however, may give thanks in the best possible way by reporting to us any keying errors that remain.

--Tom and Jerry

Chapter I

How Inputs Are Designed

So he stood a while, without thinking, feeling the cool glass on his forehead. Gradually, he became conscious of a small but persistent ticking sound in his cell.

He turned around, listening. The knocking was so quiet that at first he could not distinguish from which wall it came. While he was listening, it stopped. He started tapping himself, first on the wall over the bucket, in the direction of No. 406, but got no answer. He tried the other wall, which separated him from No. 402, next to his bed. Here he got an answer. Rubashov sat down comfortably on the bunk, from where he could keep an eye on the spy-hole, his heart beating. The first contact was always very exciting.

No. 402 was now tapping regularly; three times with short intervals, then a pause, then again three times, then again a pause, then again three times. Rubashov repeated the same series to indicate that he heard. He was anxious to find out whether the other knew the 'quadratic alphabet'--otherwise there would be a lot of fumbling until he had taught it to him. The wall was thick, with poor resonance; he had to put his head close to it to hear clearly and at the same time he had to watch the spy-hole. No. 402 had obviously had a lot of practice; he tapped distinctly and unhurriedly, probably with some hard object such as a pencil. While Rubashov was memorizing the numbers, he tried, being out of practice, to visualize the square of letters with the 25 compartments--five horizontal rows with five letters in each. No. 402 first tapped five times--accordingly the fifth row: V to Z; then twice; so it was the second letter of the row: W. Then a pause; then two taps--the second row, F-J; then three taps--the third letter of the row: H. Then three times and then five times; so fifth letter of the third row: O. He stopped.

WHO?

--Arthur Koestler, *Darkness at Noon*

Human beings are communicating animals. For those already undergoing the punishment of prison, the ultimate is "solitary confinement"--the severing of all communication. But human beings are also indominable, and the prisoner in solitary, like Koestler's Rubashov, always attempts to communicate in some way with other human beings. Usually, in spite of all efforts by the jailers of the world, he succeeds.

One of the reasons he succeeds is the human being on the other end, similarly constructed and similarly inclined to communicate. When, in modern times, we try to make contact with *computers*, in spite of all efforts by systems designers, we often fail.

The computer is like us in many ways--enough so to lull us into false confidence when we try to communicate with it. It differs from us in many other ways, not the least of which being that it is a *true* slave, not a lively human being who can take a full partnership in that wonderful, improbable, and universal act called communication.

Human beings, even when separated by a thick, poorly resonant wall, will find a way to communicate. When we work with computers, the communication pattern must be *designed* in advance--though we can design so that

human beings can participate in improving the communication, and
the computer can do its share, too.

That is what this book is about.

THE GENERATION GAP

Although computer technology has changed rapidly in the past two decades, much input design has remained in the slough of punch card thinking. This little book is an effort to stimulate the thinking of systems designers and system users to the end of bringing input design up to the level of current hardware and software--and perhaps a bit beyond.

THE KEYPUNCH GIRL

One major consequence of sterile input design is the persistence of "keypunch girl" problems. Great masses of people--almost always young women, for they are willing to work in poor conditions, at stultifying tasks, at low pay--pass large portions of their lives keying information that could be sent to the computer in ways that are more accurate, more interesting, easier, and cheaper.

Literally hundreds of millions of dollars are spent annually on this often dehumanizing activity. Only the persistence of cheap labor--available because of depressed economic conditions and the general suppression of certain groups--lets poor input design persist as its companion.

To most systems designers, this cheap labor force is essentially invisible. Of the many books now on the market concerned with "computers and society," not one even mentions this frightening waste of humanity. And, in spite of hundreds of articles on such fancy technology as interactive graphics, the vast, vast majority of computer input today is still supplied by key-driven alphanumeric devices.

These devices are operated by under-educated young women--the bottom of the social heap in present society. Engineers, doctors, stockbrokers, and various other professions dominated by the educated, male, privileged people--they are lavished with attention by systems designers.

We hope that our book will be a slight corrective to this elitist tendency, treating as it does not the exotic, but the kind of input problem borne on the backs, or fingertips, of hundreds of thousands of unsung young women.

THE VERIFICATION FALLACY

Let's take another example of the kind of design thinking--or, rather, thoughtlessness--that goes into key driven input. How many of our conventional design concepts are built around the assumption that message validity checking must be possible through "verification"?

This kind of "verification" is a euphemism for 100% repetitious keying by poor young women--keying which the designer will never see, let alone experience. We certainly don't mean to imply that systems designers have anything particular against young women. Quite likely, many of them are *for* young women. No, the verifiers are victims of a failure to move design ahead as our understanding and experience moved ahead--not to speak of our hardware and software.

OTHER "ADVANCED" FEATURES

Consider some other "advanced" design features supposedly directed at the same question--validity checking. Check digits, control sums, and limit checks are the most common techniques "beyond" repetitious keying. All these techniques come to us from an era when checking had to be carried out without reference to the file records to which their message relates.

Even though such limitations are no longer necessary, validation systems based upon them live on and on. In many shops, four generations of hardware and ten generations of designers have come and gone without making a ripple in the keypunch room--except in the sense that faster machines need more and more cards crammed in their bellies to keep them silent.

Even worse, "new" systems are designed that follow the old principles as if their designers had never heard of anything else. And perhaps they haven't.

NEW LIFE IN INPUT DESIGN

In this book we shall not attempt to rehash the ancient techniques, for they seem to be embodied in enough systems that no alert designer can fail to know them. What we wish to do, instead, is to show how new life can be put into the design of alphanumeric input systems. The search for the best message architecture must discard the view that repetitious keying is sacrosanct, or that all data must be "verified" before brought into contact with the records to which they refer.

But more than discarding old limitations to our thinking, we must conjure up new possibilities. What we must consciously include in our message design is that:

direct access to related records is the norm;

keypunch operators are human beings who will respond to design, both good and bad, in appropriate manners;

program execution speed is thousands of times faster than it was in 1955;

memories, both main and secondary, are thousands of times bigger;

the data entry process is frequently interactive;

the people who are at the source of data often understand the real world behind the data, and can be counted upon to recognize and correct many erroneous situations not accessible to the keypunch operator;

savings in the keypunch room can cause horrendous expenses in other parts of an operation--expenses that can only be eradicated by taking a broader view of the meaning of "input."

A STATE OF THE ART SURVEY

In preparation for this book, we decided to survey the companies manufacturing "input" systems. The letter shown as Figure 1.1 was sent to 26 firms which had advertised their systems in *Datamation*, *Computerworld*, *Infosystems*, and *Computer Decisions*.

ETHNOTECH, INC.

human sciences & technology

R. F. D. #2
Lincoln, Nebraska 68505
U.S.A.
(402) 781-2368

15 September 1975

Customer Relations
XYZ Corporation
East Erewhon, NJ 00000

Dear Sirs,

Tom Gilb and I are presently writing a book entitled <u>On the Design of Computer Inputs</u>, under contract with Winthrop Publishers, a subsidiary of Prentice-Hall. You may know Tom as the author of <u>Controlling the Computer</u> and <u>Reliable EDP Application Design</u>, or me as author of <u>The Psychology of Computer Programming</u> or other books on programming and systems.

We are eager to include real case studies in our book showing how modern key entry systems and specialized terminals have opened new possibilities in the design of input systems. Since your firm markets equipment for such modern systems, we are asking you to send us copies of design studies, particularly with quantitative results, showing the benefits from your approach.

If these studies prove suitably well-documented, we shall abstract them for the case studies section of our book, giving you, of course, full credit and publicity. Since we expect our book to be the standard reference for input designers, it would be a marketing plus for you to have one of your studies mentioned. Naturally, we would observe any confidential information as to source, and give credit in exactly the form you specify.

Thank you in advance for providing this information. We sincerely hope that publishing it in our book will be of mutual benefit to us, as well as to users of modern input systems.

Yours truly,

Gerald M. Weinberg

Gerald M. Weinberg
President

GMW:hs

Figure 1.1 A survey letter.

SURVEY RESPONSES

The results of our survey, in gross terms, were as follows:

One firm wrote and informed us they had gone out of business in the month since the advertisement had appeared.

One large computer company sent us a polite letter, which we intended to publish as Figure 1.2. Unfortunately attorneys advised us that this company might fear injury and go to court to stop publication of the book. Therefore we have paraphrased the letter to capture its tone and meaning, but without actually using their original words. The letter tells many things of interest to the input designer. Most important, perhaps, is that the actual use of the equipment is regarded as a pure customer problem, for which they can not or will not supply any information whatsoever. Let the buyer beware!

Dear Mr. Weinberg:

I am responding to your recent request for information.

Unfortunately, the requested information can not be supplied, as it refers to confidential or proprietary customer material.

I hope your publication enjoys great success.

Sincerely,

Controller of Communications

Figure 1.2   A paraphrase of a polite letter.

Mohawk Data Sciences sent several useful reprints of articles, plus case study information we've used later in the book.

Ball Computer Products sent us an article on the state of the art in Optical Character Recognition (OCR) systems. This article was extremely useful in establishing that proposed design ideas are valid in such systems, or in indicating when there might be supplementary considerations.

Raytheon Data Systems telephoned to determine more precisely what we needed, after which they sent exactly what we were seeking--a proposal for one of their systems. We have used the informa-

tion from this proposal in several ways, but must honor their request for confidentiality.

Entrex, Inc. sent reprints of articles, summaries of several design case studies, and a most valuable book, How to Evaluate and Select a Data Entry System. *It is our opinion that the Entrex book represents pretty much the state of the art in this area, and we recommend that potential systems designers study it in conjunction with our book, which will not attempt to duplicate the information supplied by Entrex.*

The remaining 20 companies failed to respond, though none of their letters were returned. (We did learn that another went out of business about a month later.)

WHAT WE LEARNED FROM THE SURVEY

What can we conclude from the survey itself, other than what we have gleaned from the material sent by the few companies who seem to take their business seriously?

In the first place, the data entry business is, for the most part, a *hardware selling business.* Even those companies interested in system design are heavily influenced toward the hardware side of the business, which is, after all, *their* speciality. The feeling seems to be--with justification--that the customer knows *his* business better than they ever could, so the design of actual input is done only in the broadest outlines.

Secondly, the data entry business is a *volatile* business--at least at the present time. Two out of 26 firms went out of business in one two-month interval, and we have no way of knowing how many more started up. There is a similar volatility in the products themselves, with new features appearing regularly--accompanied by glittering announcements.

To the customer, this volatility means preparation for changed hardware as components are added to the system.   The input designs must be *portable*.   To us, the writers of a book on input design, it means that our lessons must transcend particular hardware features and touch upon deep, invariant principles of input design.

For these reasons, we shall restrict our discussion of input design to the "soft" parts, and touch upon hardware only when differences in hardware might be relevant to design choices concerning "software." By software, here, we mean not so much the computer programs, but the messages themselves--the information flowing between people and computers.

HOW WE GOT WHERE WE ARE TODAY

It's difficult to keep hardware from creeping into input design.   For one thing, we've been using hardware so long that most system designers have little idea what things were like before Herman Hollerith brought the punch card down from the mountaintop. For that reason, we want to sketch an evolution that brought us where we are today, as a prelude to some thoughts about where we will be tomorrow.

THE ONE-PERSON BUSINESS

Consider the one-person business--a shoe-shine stand on Wall Street, a candy store in St. Joe, a telephone company in Virgin, Utah.   The information system for such a firm is likely to resemble that shown in Figure 1.3.

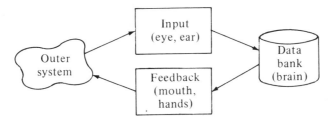

Figure 1.3   The information system of a small firm.

The "hardware" in this system is the human body. The input is the eyes and ears; the output, the mouth and hands. The memory is the brain, and the software is thoughts.

In such a system, the programming is completely automatic and implicit. Messages are in simple, natural English. Explicit design doesn't exist, or hardly exists. Everything is in the owner-operator's head. When the owner dies, the business dies, too.

THE BUSINESS GROWS

In order to provide continuity in such a business, or to meet legal or tax requirements, or to allow for growth by the addition of employees, written records are created. Procedures and design may still be implicit and adaptive, but no one person any longer has immediate access to all information about the business.

As more people become involved, explicit procedures must be created to consolidate scattered information for guiding the business. The paper information no longer represents the "outer system"--the real world--very accurately. Information is out of date. Transcription introduces errors. Consolidation amalgamates sources of varying reliability and differential timeliness. Eventually, machines are introduced to improve management's *image* of the firm--since the firm itself is essentially unknowable.

MECHANIZING INFORMATION

In mechanization, up to now, there were three great stages:

mechanical handling of unitized records--the punch card with sorters, collators, and tabulating machines.

programming of procedures--eliminating human handling steps in moving from one machine to another.

memory--crudely, at first, with punch cards, a few registers, and then tape, but now rapidly advancing in a variety of directions with "random access" memories.

The first of these stages, unitized records, introduced the keypunch between the real world and the data bank. From that moment, layer upon layer of machinery and procedures was added to counteract some limitation of the card unit record. In the end, the layers themselves came to be "the system" to most of us. In a typical system, *why* is lost in a maze of *how*, as in Figure 1.4, below.

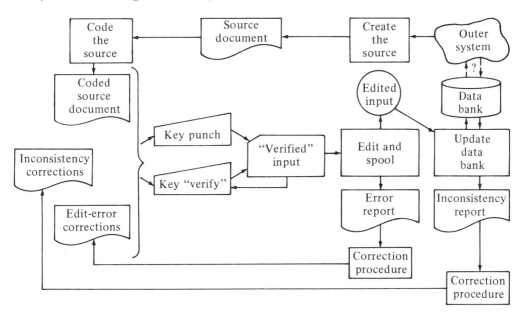

Figure 1.4 Typical punch card based input system
         (idealized and simplified).

Yet beneath those layers, somewhere, is an attempt to capture the immediacy and precision of the one-person system of Figure 1.3.

PEELING BACK THE LAYERS

In the past, design meant adding layers between the system and its image. Now, more and more, it means stripping them off.

Programming and *memory* are now being applied--at long, long last--to the problem of peeling back the layers made necessary by the unitization of records with punch cards. In many cases, programming and memory could long ago have been applied to these problems. New input devices merely provide the missing impetus. In other cases, programming and memory could not have improved the situation until new machines were available to replace the keypunch, and new media, the card.

KEYPUNCH REPLACEMENT DESIGNS

The most common approach to applying new hardware might be called "keypunch replacement." Figure 1.5 shows a typical keypunch replacement system.

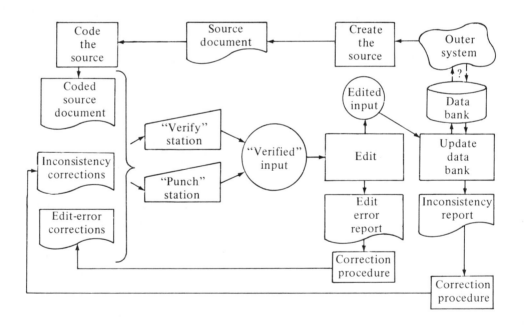

Figure 1.5 Typical keypunch replacement system
(idealized and simplified).

ATTRIBUTES

A system like that in Figure 1.5 may improve the input situation by one or more of the following:

> *duplicating*
>
> *zero, space, or constant filling*
>
> *skipping or tabbing*
>
> *emitting constant information*
>
> *incrementing*
>
> *keyboard shifting*
>
> *right or left justifying*
>
> *programming for multiple formats*
>
> *prompting the operator*

In addition, various checking operations might be programmed into the key-entry device--operations that were formerly not done, or done only at edit time. In the simplest cases, however, the first step is an "improved" replacement of the keypunch, so that key verification and all editing programs are preserved.

Additional savings may accrue from elimination of card handling between punch and key verify, from elimination of a separate "spooling" run to transfer cards to tape, from reduced card stock costs, or from tabulation of batch totals within the key entry device.

IMPACT

Direct replacement can sometimes be done without affecting other parts of the system--which may not even be informed of the change of key entry device. The situation is not so clean when the change slices into deeper layers.

Even the change from key verification to sight verification--which seems like a direct replacement-- can have far-reaching effects. Though sight verification may lead to a gross reduction in input errors, certain *classes* of error may show an increase in contrast to repetitive keying. These errors impinging on the edit programs may lead to

> *discovery of program paths not previously traversed.*
>
> *exposure of errors in these paths.*
>
> *new kinds of messages and situations for the correction procedures.*
>
> *some errors slipping through into the update programs.*
>
> *some errors reaching the data bank itself.*

A number of installations have been surprised by this kind of change in what they thought was a direct replacement situation. In designing for the transit- ion, allowance should be made for the effects of alter- ed error characteristics.

FRONT-END REPLACEMENT

As we deviate further and further from direct re- placement of keypunches, we must anticipate more and more effects on the system as a whole. The net result may be beneficial, but new situations are always more discouraging if we imagined everything would be uni- formly "better" under the new system. In Figure 1.6, we see what might be called a "front-end" replacement system--another attempt to replace keypunching with minimal impact elsewhere in the system.

ATTRIBUTES

The front-end replacement peels off the separate layers of the system aimed at editing and replaces them with a single layer. This step takes advantage of the programming possibilities of the input station and, to some extent, its memory. Front-end replace- ment, however, does not use memory in the sense of checking for consistency with the data bank.

A common use of such a front-end system is in systems with several remote input sources. Each

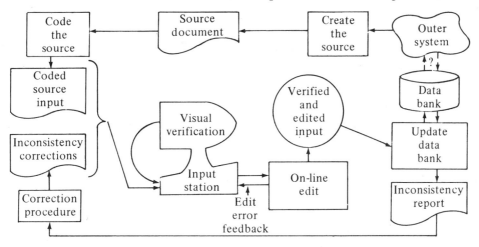

Figure 1.6   Typical front-end replacement input
system (idealized and simplified).

source is given an input station with editing capabilities, which reduces the need for transmitting error
information back and forth between source and central
data bank. Such a system can reduce turnaround time
on many transactions, and slash the cost of error
correction. It will, however, require reprogramming
the editing previously done at the central computing
facility.

IMPACT

Though many installations have tried, it is generally impossible to duplicate the old edit routine
precisely on the input station hardware. We may not
even *want* to duplicate it precisely--we will probably
be tempted to improve it.

If we yield to temptation, we can still control
the resultant disturbances by keeping the old central
edit program in operation after the installation of
the remote stations, as suggested in Figure 1.7.

In this design, if the central edit programs are
in fact duplicated, we will see an empty error listing
from the central edit program. Nevertheless, the added protection will generally pay off in one of the

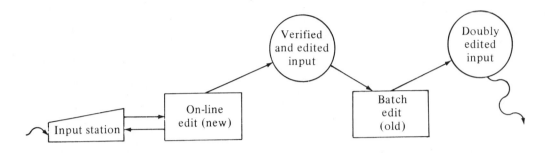

Figure 1.7   Interposing the old edit program
between the new edit and the update.

following ways:

*By taking the pressure off the programming of the
remote stations, we may get more reliable work in
the first place.*

*By permitting incremental development of the re-
mote editing programs, we can spread the cost of
programming and avoid overstaffing.*

*By preventing havoc in the central computing fac-
ility, we help out at a time when other changes
may be keeping everyone busy.*

*By retaining the error listing, we give a stand-
ard against which the performance of the remote
stations can be measured.*

ON-LINE BATCHED UPDATE INPUT

A much more drastic system change is seen in
Figure 1.8, where everything standing between the key
input and the update has been replaced by a single on-
line edit and update program.

ATTRIBUTES

The advantage of this system is that editing can
be done in relation to the existing data bank, permit-

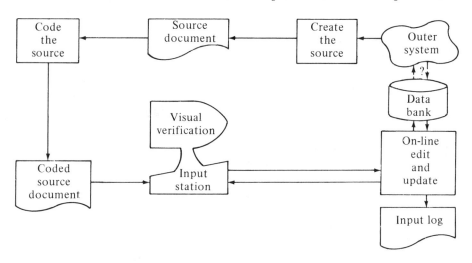

Figure 1.8   Typical on-line batched update input
                     (idealized and simplified)

ting such techniques as

> *checking on the actual existence of a given rec-
> ord in the data bank, rather than simple legality
> of an identifier.*

> *presenting information from the data bank to ver-
> ify that the appropriate record is chosen.*

> *preventing transactions that might be legal, but
> actually aren't for this particular case, such as
> overdrafts, exceeding credit limits, or security
> violations.*

Many other advantages could be given, but perhaps
the greatest of all is the ability to correct all detectable errors before modifying the data bank.   Errors that penetrate the data bank can prove surpassing-
ly expensive to remove, so a gram of prevention is
worth a kilogram of cure.

IMPACT

Many editing situations, as we hope to demonstrate later in this book, are *easier to program* when the
data bank is available at the time of editing.   And,
working in cooperation with an intelligent operator,

programs to make corrections can often be trivial exercises.

Nevertheless, going on-line from a batch system is bound to engender complications. Providing for these complications is one of the main tasks of the system designer, and *ease of implementation* must include not only programming problems, but also problems of changeover from a different, more familiar system-- no matter how poorly it might be designed.

ELIMINATION OF CODING STEPS

When our input system goes on-line error correction should prove simpler and faster, in both human and machine terms. Unfortunately, if we concentrate on varieties of hardware replacement, this potential ease may not be realized.

CODING AND ERRORS

One major stumbling block is the coded form of the input material. When separate coding steps intervene between source and key entry, the person making the entry may lack the information needed to make a correction, for one or more of the following reasons:

The error may be in the coding itself.

The original source may have had redundant information in one item that could have been used to correct another item, but is lost in coding.

The original item itself may have redundancy not found in the coded form, and this redundancy can help in the correction.

WHY ARE WE CODING?

Of course, coding is an *extra* step, and thus costs extra time and money. The system designer must ask:

Why are we coding in the first place?

In reply to this question, the designer may discover such origins as these:

The coding was necessary to reduce the number of input columns to fit on one card.

The coding eliminated certain characters that old equipment couldn't handle, or couldn't handle economically.

The coding placed variable-length items into fixed fields, which were necessary for processing on the former equipment.

The coding expanded abbreviated information, which couldn't have been done on equipment without memory.

The coding categorized a variety of cases into a single code, which couldn't have been done without processing ability in the equipment.

The coding involved some arithmetic, which again would have required processing abilities.

ATTRIBUTES

An examination of the origins of coding will generally reveal that all coding can now be done by the computer, at least once the updating is on-line. Even when the main data bank is inaccessible to the entry system, most coding can be done by a reasonably "intelligent" key station.

Sometimes it will seem that coding will "reduce keystrokes"--a sub-goal often mistaken for the main objective of input design. While it is true that coding done in another department may reduce keystrokes in the data preparation area, the economy for the entire organization will virtually always be a false one. Not only is the coding a slower process than most keying, but each additional transcription increases the chance of error, while decreasing the chance of a simple correction of that error.

Such analysis will lead designers to eliminate many, if not all, coding operations. At worst, coding

might be done during the initial creation of the
source document. Slightly better might be coding at
the entry station--where a real savings in time might
result, but where coding errors can be immediately
signalled and corrected with the source document at
hand. In such systems, we may see a simplified flow
of input such as shown in Figure 1.9.

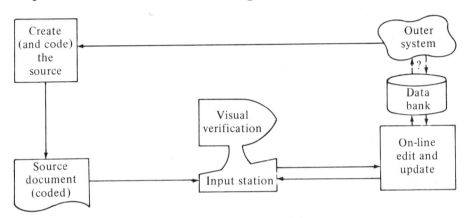

Figure 1.9   Eliminating or consolidating the
coding step.

In other systems, we may see the elimination of coding
before the updating actually goes on-line, or even at
the front-end replacement stage.

IMPACT

In some systems, coding will be eliminated entirely. In others, coding will be reduced, or changed,
or displaced to more appropriate stations.

Though great gains in performance can be obtained
by eliminating or consolidating coding, these possibilities are frequently overlooked in current input
design practice. Probably, they wouldn't result in
direct replacement of machine cost, and might even
show an increased cost in the data preparation area.
Thoughtful analysis, however, will usually demonstrate
that savings in error-correction activity will, in
themselves, pay for increased "keystrokes"--without
even counting the savings in other cost centers.

Nevertheless, whenever a change originating in the data processing department flows outside that department--even at great reduction of total effort--great delicacy will be needed to effect the transition. We shall have a great deal to say, later on, concerning the design of input systems that eliminate or consolidate coding steps.

CLOSING THE LOOP

Once a design has reached the stage of development represented by Figure 1.9, it becomes relatively easy to perceive the remaining layer between the actual system and its image in the data bank. That layer is the "source" document itself. Figure 1.10 shows the evolution come full circle, with the system's users in direct contact for both input and output--more or less at will.

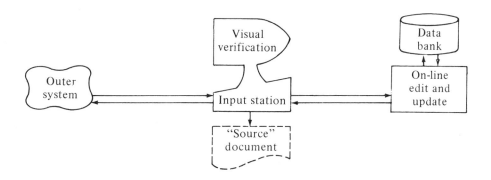

Figure 1.10   Closing the loop between data bank and outer system.

ATTRIBUTES

A "source" document may be produced in a closed-loop system--for auditing purposes, for legal requirements, or perhaps just for old times' sake. But now it's an *output*, not an input. It represents an actual transaction accepted and carried out by the system,

not a potential transaction that will be carried out
if it passes a series of screening steps.

IMPACT

The immediacy of such a system is clearly one of
its major advantages. Errors are prevented, rather
than detected and corrected. All parts of the data
bank can be kept in synchronization, without elaborate
procedures to correct for the variable delays of batch
processing. Users need not be kept in Limbo, waiting
to discover if their transaction is acceptable, only
to be disappointed after a long delay.

But faster ain't necessarily better. In some
systems, the users have *adapted* to the batching delays
in ways that will make them suffer from immediate response. Although the long run may be a balm to this
initial suffering, the system must live through the
short run if there is to be a long run at all. More
than one on-line system has capsized because it changed
its users' world too quickly in ways they hadn't anticipated.

THE ADVANTAGE OF BACKWARDNESS

In many ways, it would have been simpler to skip
the card phase and go directly to on-line systems.
Numerous organizations are doing just that, reaping
the rewards of what anthropologists call "the advantage of backwardness." These people will be designing
their systems without so much to unlearn, but they
will still have much to learn. We hope to teach them
much of what they need to know that the hardware ven-
dors will not be able to teach them.

For the vast majority of input designers, however,
a goodly proportion of the work will be stripping away
layers no longer mandated by equipment limitations.
This will leave them free to concentrate on the human
aspects of the human-computer interface, possibly for
the first time in their careers. This new freedom
carries new responsibilities--an obligation to think
in new ways. We must brush out the cobwebs of

machine-influenced designs and to start learning about
the communicating animal for whose benefit all other
systems are supposed to be designed.

Chapter II

Default Messages

He had fourty-two boxes, all carefully packed,
    With his name painted carefully on each:
But, since he omitted to mention the fact,
    They were all left behind on the beach.

The loss of his clothes hardly mattered, because
    He had seven coats on when he came,
With three pairs of boots--but the worst of it was,
    He had wholly forgotten his name.

--The Hunting of the Snark, Fit the First

Alas, the poor forgetful Baker, if he only understood
about defaults--what you get when you forget (or just
decline) to mention some fact. Yet all of us, input
operators included, are a bit limited mentally, which
is why *default* input is one of the simplest design
techniques. From the operator's point of view, there
is no direct effort, either physical or mental, to key
in the data. With proper design, the operator may be
saved from any explicit action to indicate missing
input, such as skipping a field or inserting a zero or
blank.

The default technique can ordinarily be expected to reduce input errors, based on the simple idea that *what you don't do you can't do wrong.* In COBOL, using the form

ADD QUANTITY TO TOTAL-QUANTITY.

requires fewer keystrokes and reduces the chances for error over

ADD QUANTITY TO TOTAL-QUANTITY GIVING TOTAL-QUANTITY.

Nevertheless, no technique is powerful enough to help if you "forget your name"--the operator must contribute something, no matter how well the system is backed up with boots and coats.

THE PSYCHOLOGY OF DEFAULT MESSAGES

Defaults are used so frequently in ordinary discourses and commerce that we hardly notice them as a technique at all, yet they must be considered as a valid design alternative in almost every message design situation.

DEFAULTS IN NATURAL LANGUAGE

Consider the set of English sentences:

1. *John drove to the grocery store and John bought a loaf of bread.*

2. *John drove to the store and John bought a loaf of bread.*

3. *John drove to the store and bought a loaf of bread.*

4. *John drove to the store and bought bread.*

5. *John drove and bought bread.*

6. *John bought bread.*

7. *John.*

8. *(pause)*

9. *(nothing at all)*

The first sentence expresses the full message explicitly. Sentence (2) takes advantage of the fact that either:

We *know* that bread is bought at the *grocery* store.

We *don't care* precisely what store was involved.

In either case, the message can be shortened because of *information available to the recipient.*

Sometimes the recipient's information is *internal.* In passing from sentence (2) to sentence (3), we eliminate the repetition of "John" because of the internal structuring of defaults in English, which the recipient presumably knows. Passing from (3) to (4), we eliminate "a loaf of" on the basis of a *standard default quantity.* From (4) to (5) we can eliminate "to the store" by using a standard default *location of purchase*; while from (5) to (6) we make use of a standard default *means of transportation.* Each of these defaults would be appropriate in a commercial environment, as we shall see.

In passing from (6) to (7), we may employ the idea of a *standard question,* to which only one variable element--the name of the person who drove to the grocery store and bought a loaf of bread--needs to be added. From (7) to (8), we need only signify by a pause (or a carriage return or end of record) that the standard action was taken, by the standard person. And, finally, in passing from (8) to (9), we eliminate even the need for a control character or a pause by simply not asking the question--under the assumption that if there were some deviation from the default pattern, we would certainly be informed.

NATURALNESS OF DEFAULTS

Notice, incidentally, that when we *fail* to use such defaults in ordinary discourse, it seems queer to others. Suppose you ask the question:

> *Did John drive to the grocery store and buy a loaf of bread?*

and your listener responds:

> *John drove to the grocery store and John bought a loaf of bread.*

instead of a simple *"yes"* or nod of the head. A few responses of this type and you would become convinced that your listener was mentally ill, and indeed this kind of response pattern is often a sign of certain mental afflictions. Therefore, it is not surprising that computer input systems that fail to make use of *natural* defaults often force their users to feel ill at ease, for they must behave in a manner that would, among humans, indicate social awkwardness, if not actual mental problems.

EXAMPLE: ORDER ENTRY OF ELECTRONIC PARTS

Imagine an order entry system which receives the following two order messages:

	CUSTOMER I.D.	*SHIP VIA*	*QTY*	*PRODUCT CODE*
(1)	CHWY	SURFACE	234	XP197
			313	ZT39
(2)	JONCO		6	JG4889
				JG338

Some of the defaults in these messages are quite obvious, such as carrying the customer identification through all elements of the order. Indeed, this is so natural an interpretation that we ordinarily fail to notice it at all, which may lead to some troubles in our system design.

FILLING IN GLOBAL DEFAULTS

The various line items on the order may have to be separated for internal processing, in which case each *internal* line may need to have a great deal of default information filled in--information that didn't appear with that line item in the input.

For instance, the different text lines in the above example might have to be separated by the program, and possibly sorted into one or more new sequences. When such a separation is made, the program must attach the explicit representation of the default option to each of the individual product line orders. Otherwise, separate processing would be impossible. Such sorting might be required if the products were needed in product number sequence for such activities as:

sequential file access, or faster direct access

overall inventory evaluation before any orders are executed

a product picking list for the warehouse, with all orders picked at once to minimize labor.

LOCAL CONDITIONAL DEFAULTS

The shipping method may similarly be carried through into each line, but an even further default can be seen. In order (1), there is a message indicating that the order is to be sent by *surface* mail, but order (2) also contains a message about shipping. It is to be sent by *AIR MAIL*.

We avoided writing *AIR MAIL* explicitly to save the effort and eliminate chances for error. In this case, 98% of our electronic reserve parts are automatically sent by the fastest method, though it is possible to indicate other modes of shipment when desired. *AIR MAIL* is the default option for this type of part, which everybody working with the system normally knows through training, common sense, experience, or feedback from the system.

Alternatively, the operator may *not* know that *AIR MAIL* is the default. Determining the most economical or fastest method of shipment may be a calculation involving a variety of factors, and best left to the computer unless explicitly overridden. There simply may be no reason for the operator to know the method of shipment on all orders.

QUANTIFICATION EXAMPLE: THE ONE DOZEN ORDER

How much is a particular default design worth? How much keying does it save, and what effect does it have on the rate of erroneous items entering the system? Several examples will illustrate some of the design computations that can be done concerning defaults.

A wholesale drug company takes orders in units, but most of their orders are for an even dozen--which is the typical quantity in which the items are packed. We want to consider four design alternatives for entering the quantity:

a. *fixed field of 3 positions, no defaults*

b. *variable field of up to 3 positions, plus one trailing blank as separator, no defaults*

c. *fixed field as in (a), but with one dozen defaulting to blank.*

d. *variable field, as in (b), but with default as in (c).*

The following table shows the four methods in use-- with (a) and (b) designating 5 of item X37, and (c) and (d) designating 12 of item R43

(a)	(b)	(c)	(d)
005X37	5b̸X37	b̸b̸b̸R43	R43
b̸b̸5X37		ⱦ R43	12b̸R43
5ⱦ X37		012R43	

("b̸" represents a stroke on the space key and "ⱦ" represents a stroke on the tab (skip) key).

THE FREQUENCY DISTRIBUTION

In order to compute the amount of keying under each method, we shall first need the *frequency distribution* of the different quantities. For instance, we may find (by sampling existing orders) that 12 occurs 85% of the time. One-digit order quantities, 1-9, appear 5% of the time. For present analytical purposes, only number of digits counts, so we need not refine the distribution further within this class of one-digit numbers. Two-digit items (other than 12) account for 9% of the orders, and the remaining 1% of the orders are 3 digits long.

We can fill these cases and their frequencies in a table such as Figure 2.1, leaving one column for the keystrokes needed under each method. Method (a) requires three key strokes for a 12, including the two digits and a leading zero, a space, or a skip to fill out the fixed field (012, 12ɓ, or 12ʈ).

Two strokes are needed in method (a) for single digits (3ʈ)--if the operator can and does use the skip key instead of the two spaces for filling the field, and if the decimal points need not be aligned.

Input case	Frequency (f)	METHOD							
		(a) Fixed field no default		(b) Var. field no default		(c) Fixed field default		(d) Var. field default	
		s	f X s	s	f X s	s	f X s	s	f X s
12 (dozen)	.85	3	2.55	3	2.55	1	.85	0	.00
1-digit	.05	2	.10	2	.10	2	.10	2	.10
2-digit (≠12)	.09	3	.27	3	.27	3	.27	3	.27
3-digit	.01	3	.03	4	.04	3	.03	4	.04
Average keystrokes per entry		2.95		2.96		1.25		.41	

Figure 2.1 Estimated keystrokes under four designs of a quantity input (s = number of keystrokes required, including skip or left zero adjustment)

COMPUTING KEYING EFFORT

We note that method (b) actually requires slightly more effort, since a three-digit number requires a blank following the digits to separate the fields (123ɓ). As a result, variable fields are actually slightly worse than fixed fields for this application --without defaults.

When we use defaults for the case of 12, the situation is dramatically different. With fixed fields (method c), one stroke is needed to skip the field. With variable fields, *no* stroke is needed, since the separator from the previous field does the job.

Although variable field again requires an additional stroke for the longest case, this case is so infrequent that the effect on the overall keying rate is minimal. Because of the differences between 0 and 1 strokes for the most frequent case, the average number of strokes goes down from 1.2 to 0.4. Either case is a considerable saving over the 3.0 of the non-default design--a factor of 3/0.4, or a factor of 7.5.

DESIGN ASSUMPTIONS

In any design, we make a number of assumptions. When the design is implemented, these assumptions--when inaccurate--will lead to discrepancies between the design calculations and the achieved figures. The designer is responsible not only for the design, but for unearthing the assumptions that may prove critical to its success or failure.

Assumptions that prove wrong don't necessarily prove bad. The design might just as well perform *better* than expected, because of something we overlooked. In general, however, because of the sales-oriented environment in which most input designs are made, assumptions do tend to be optimistic rather than pessimistic. Therefore, designers who bury their assumptions are more likely to get a nasty surprise than a pleasant one.

THE COMPOSITION FALLACY

One of the most commonly wrong design assumptions is what is called the *Composition Fallacy* (see Weinberg, 1975). The Composition Fallacy assumes that the whole is exactly equal to the sum of its parts. A common example of this fallacy is the assumption that a team's performance will be determined strictly by the skills of the individual members, which is rarely true.

In data entry, the Composition Fallacy states, for one thing, that actual keying rates for the whole application will equal the sum of the rates for all individual fields. In reality, overall rates are rarely determinable with precision from the individual rates.

Certain keys or combinations are faster than others. The order of fields in the input relative to their order on source documents, or relative to their "natural" order, will affect the total keying rate. These and a myriad of other factors combine to make it foolish to rely on more than order-of-magnitude estimates of keying rates. Nevertheless, a reduction of *about* 7 to 1 will probably mean considerable savings, and might turn out to be 10 to 1. Then again, it could turn out to be 5 to 1, so be prepared!

ASSUMPTIONS ABOUT ERROR RATES

Even more important in most applications is the effect that defaults have on *error* rates. The initial assumption is that all keystrokes have the same error probability. Though this approximation is certainly crude, it leads to the estimate that errors will be reduced in the same proportion as keystrokes are reduced. This is a reasonable assumption in many situations, and a 7 to 1 reduction in errors entering the first stage of the system is bound to have a salutary effect on costs and operating conditions.

Even so, the error reduction could be even greater if the new procedure is more "comfortable" for the operators. Or, to look at the dark side, an "uncomfortable" procedure may increase errors. And, since any *new* procedure is bound to be a bit uncomfortable, the designer had better be prepared for the error rate to be somewhat higher than estimates at the onset.

As the operators become familiar with the new procedure, we can expect the error rate to diminish--even-
tually converging to something *close* to our estimate,
hopefully.

MOTIVATIONAL ASSUMPTIONS

One other assumption that cannot be left unmen-
tioned is the motivation of the operators. Even
before keypunches, typewriters were sometimes affixed
with counters to measure the "productivity" of typists
--the number of keystrokes. When motivated by this
measurement, the operators increased the number of
keystrokes per day. The industrial engineers proudly
watched the "productivity" rise, as they knew, by
force of scientific law--it must. Their pride in
their "achievement" blinded them all the longer to the
actual facts of the matter. Operators *never* used the
tabulator key, and rather frequently spaced out, one
stroke at a time, to the right-hand margin. Depending
on how the counters were rigged, they adopted other
stratagems, such as backspace-space combinations to
bring them up to their quota of "productivity."

In our example, we shall not realize the potential of the "skip" key if the operators are motivated
to produce as many keystrokes as possible. Indeed,
we may find them ignoring the default possibilities
altogether. Only by improving our concept of "productivity" will we achieve the full potential improvement of our design. Counting *finished* work--with
appropriate adjustment for the value of reliable work
--will be more likely to give the kind of motivation
we need for our design to succeed. And, of course,
any environmental improvement that makes the operators
identify their interests with the organization's interests will only add to that success.

SENSITIVITY TO ASSUMPTIONS

In any design, *conscious* assumptions that fail could
cause as much trouble as unconscious ones. When the

assumptions are explicit, however, we are not entirely at their mercy. By performing *sensitivity* studies, we can discover which assumptions, if any, need to be refined.

THE AXIOM OF EXPERIENCE

For example, a common explicit assumption is the *frequency distribution* of the various input categories. In Figure 2.1, we evaluate four designs based on a particular distribution which we might write as:

f = (.85, .05, .09, .01)

These numbers are *predictions* about the future, and therefore constitute *assumptions*, for nobody can *know* the future.

Too often, designers fail to realize that such frequency distributions are indeed assumptions. Some designers are misled by the *appearance of precision*. Others "know" the distribution is correct because it is based on past experience. Yet the value of experience is contingent on an article of faith, which we may call *the Axiom of Experience* (Weinberg, 1975):

*The future will be like the past, because,
in the past, the future was like the past.*

More than one system surprised its designers when the future changed--perhaps in reaction to the system itself.

FAMILIES OF VALUES

One way to reduce the number of surprises is to study how the design will perform *if the assumptions do not hold*. In the case of quantitative assumptions, such a sensitivity study is relatively straightforward. We begin by developing a mathematical relationship of the dependence of the design on the various assumptions, treated as parameters. Then, instead of studying a single set of values, as in Figure 2.1, we study *families* of sets of values.

For instance, we may study the family of values of the frequency distribution, F, designated by

F = (x, .05, .09, y)

where x is the frequency of dozen orders and y is the frequency of 3-digit orders--the best and worst cases for our default designs. This family, described in words, is

> *All those frequency distributions in which the*
> *1-digit items constitute 5% of all items and*
> *the 2-digit items (excluding an even dozen)*
> *constitute 9% of all items.*

LIMITING CASES

The distribution in Figure 2.1 is *one member* of this family. Other members include

f_1 = (0, .05, .09, .86)

and

f_2 = (.86, .05, .09, 0)

These two members, in fact, represent *extreme* members of the family, or limiting cases. Limiting cases are important because they set bounds on how good, or how bad, each design can be with respect to the assumed parameters.

PARAMETRIC PLOTS

Another way of appreciating the effect of the parameters is to plot the reaction of each design to each family. In Figure 2.2, we see how the designs (c) and (d) are affected by changes in the percentages of dozen and 3-digit entries. Design (d) has lower

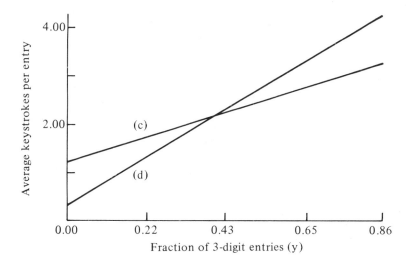

Figure 2.2   Sensitivity of the designs to the distribution of input categories, in the family (x, .05, .09, y)

average keystrokes up to the family member

$$f_3 = (.40, .05, .09, .46)$$

at which point, the two lines cross.

In other words, the two designs would be equivalent (with respect to keystrokes) if the actual distribution were f_3. This family member is rather far away from our best assumed distribution,

$$f = (.85, .05, .09, .01)$$

so the design choice is *not very sensitive* to variation in the fraction of dozen entries--as long as our original guess was reasonably stable. Had the original distribution been predicted at

$$f_3 = (.40, .05, .09, .46)$$

the choice of design would have been *maximally sensitive* to variation. In such a case, it would probably be profitable to invest some time and money in refining the assumed value of F.

PLOTTING THE IMPORTANCE OF MOTIVATION

Another assumption buried in Figure 2.1 is that defaults and other stroke-shortening devices will be used at the maximum possible level. As we have seen, this assumption may not be satisfied, at least when the design is new to the operators. The sensitivity to this assumption can be modeled, based on a parameter giving the fraction of the time the operators actually use the dozen default.

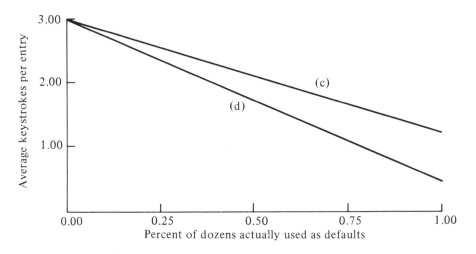

Figure 2.3   Sensitivity of the designs to the
             actual use of defaults by the
             operators.

Figure 2.3 shows a graph of keystrokes versus this parameter for designs (c) and (d). As the graph shows clearly, there is little reason to choose (d) over (c) unless the operators will actually use the default-- thus confirming what we believed intuitively. The graph also enables us to estimate the value of a certain amount of training or motivation. In conjunction with a learning curve, it enables us to predict the rate at which keystrokes will diminish with experience.

QUANTIFICATION EXAMPLE: THE REFERENCE NUMBER/WORD

A manufacturer of precision equipment, in its order
entry system, has two kinds of authorization reference
numbers. For government and military--the bulk of
their business--there is a 7-character "number,"
mostly alphabetic information of a mnemonic nature.
For orders originating elsewhere, there is a 4-digit
number, of no particular structure. In their original
system, a field of 7 positions is set aside for this
information, with the final 3 positions simply left
blank when a 4-digit number is entered.

TAKING ADVANTAGE OF STRUCTURE

In a review of their system, the designers noticed
that most customers--including individual agencies of
the government--used the *same* reference number for *all*
their orders. In fact, something like 94% of all authorization reference numbers given on the forms were a
reference number that could have been kept as a constant in the customer record. In these cases, because
the customer record would be available on-line in the
new system, only the customer number was needed. An
explicit reference number had to be keyed only if it
deviated from the conventional one displayed to the
operator.

In the new design, a blank reference number field
signified the default--use the reference number in the
customer record. Given the frequencies of the various
cases, the designers could estimate the performance of
the new system by constructing a table such as shown
in Figure 2.4

KEYSTROKE ESTIMATES

Under the old system, 5 keystrokes were needed
for the 4-digit numbers, whether or not they were derivable from other information. For example:

4773¢   019A¢   RTST¢

Input case		Frequency (f)	METHOD							
			Explicit				Default			
			keystrokes		errors/1000		keystrokes		errors/1000	
# of digits	def?		s	f × s	n	f × n	s	f × s	n	f × n
4		.01	5	.05	10	.10	5	.05	10	.10
4	yes	.36	5	1.80	10	3.60	1	.36	—	—
7		.05	7	.35	3	.15	7	.35	3	.15
7	yes	.58	7	4.06	3	1.74	1	.58	—	—
Averages			6.26		5.59		1.34		.25	

Figure 2.4   Performance of reference "numbers"
with and without defaults.

Seven strokes were needed for the government numbers, as in

MILBAL3   MILELEC   STDSNTS

Under the old system, therefore, an average of
6.3 keystrokes were required per entry. Under the
proposed fixed-field default system, this number was
estimated to fall to 1.3 keystrokes--a reduction of
4.7 to 1.

ERROR ESTIMATES

In this case, however, the raw keystroke reduction was too crude a measure of the reduction of
errors. Because of the arbitrary nature of the 4-
digit number, errors were experienced at the rate of
10 per 1000 entries. The longer code, being more
mnemonic, actually had a much smaller error rate--
about 3 per 1000. The humanization of such codes is
a subject for another part of the book, but for the
moment we wish to observe that the average errors per
1000 transactions overall under the old system was
about 5.6--a number reduced to .25 under the default
design. This reduction in error rate of 22 to 1 is
much greater than suggested by the simple reduction

in keying rate. Consequently, we cannot always use the keystroke rate to estimate errors--at least if high accuracy is required in the estimate.

TRANSMISSION ESTIMATES

It should also be noticed that keystroke estimates cannot always be used to estimate transmission effort between terminal and central computer, since one character keyed does not always produce one character transmitted. Under fixed-field systems, such as punch cards or terminal systems modelled after them, the number of characters transmitted does not depend on the *contents* of a field. In this design, for instance, the average keystrokes were 1.3 to produce a transmission of 7 characters--most often all blanks. If, on the other hand, a variable field design were used, keystrokes could be reduced to .45, and transmission would be reduced in exactly the same proportion. Thus, if transmission load is important, variable fields might be selected even if the reduction in keystrokes were insignificant.

FEEDBACK OF DEFAULTS

When the operator does need to know the consequences of default actions, it may be good input design to provide an explicit statement. In our order entry example, the system specification could call for the program to display--on a suitable device--a *feedback* message such as:

AIR SHIPMENT ASSUMED SINCE NO OTHER INDICATED

The advantage of feedback is in making the operator aware of the consequences of default actions. While this may be done purely for training, it will ordinarily safeguard against unintentional defaults. Therefore, the feedback system will normally provide the operator an opportunity for self-correction before continuing, after having seen that the intended message was not communicated.

For instance, we might see the following message protocol:

JONC 6 JG4889   JG338

<u>AIR SHIPMENT SINCE NO OTHER INDICATED</u>

SURFACE

<u>SHIPMENT OPTION CHANGED TO SURFACE FOR JONC ORDER</u>

(When presenting dialogues between a person and a machine, we will follow the convention of *underlining* the machine's contribution, as above.)

THE DEFAULT ORDER QUANTITY

This example illustrates another variation of a default input. In an ordering system where the quantity "one" occurs on a large percentage of all order lines, the message design may allow the system to assume the quantity "one," just as we saw it could do with the quantity 12. In other applications, the *same* quantity may not prevail for each item, but each item might have its *own* characteristic ordering quantity-- a *loaf* of bread, a *dozen* eggs, a *ream* (500 sheets) of paper, and so forth. In the days when internal storage was limited and direct access devices were only a gleam in their inventor's eye, a separate default for each item would have been uneconomical. Today, it may prove an efficient solution.

TRAINING THROUGH FEEDBACK

In such instances, it would certainly be good practice to use feedback to train the operators, not only to show what defaults have been taken, but to show when they *might* have taken a default, but didn't. For instance, we can imagine the following protocol:

JONC 6 JG4889 JG338

AIR SHIPMENT ASSUMED

ONE JG338 ASSUMED

NOTE: SIX IS THE DEFAULT ORDER FOR JG4889

AND NEED NOT BE GIVEN!

If the word NOTE is made sufficiently conspicuous to the operator, subsequent entries for JG4889 might be made using the default quantity of 6. Since 6 is a rather unusual default in this application (most of the items are packed 4, 10, or 12 to a box, or kept singly), it is unlikely that most operators will learn to use it without some sort of operational feedback. Through such feedback, the experienced operator gradually, painlessly, and without cost, learns to enter information more speedily, more accurately, and in a manner that is more comfortable and satisfying.

ALLOWING EXPLICIT EXPRESSION OF DEFAULT OPTIONS

As the preceeding example implies, it should normally be possible to express default options explicitly if the operator so desires. The operator might be unsure, initially, of what each default option is. Sometimes we have operators who do not use the system often enough to learn the defaults. Psychologically, it may be easier to enter the quantity desired than to take the "risk" of guessing wrong, even though the system has (hopefully) been designed to protect against error either way.

ZIPF'S LAW

We may reasonably assume that with feedback, the operator will learn to take advantage of the efficiencies offered by the default options. Most people will act in such a way as to shorten messages they must use repeatedly. An empirical observation in linguistics, Zipf's Law, indicates that the most commonly used words and grammatical forms in a language come, over time, to be the shortest. We can quite accurately predict that a word such as "I" is rather frequently used in English, and that "necessitarianism" is not-- or, rather, "isn't."

This shortening process will generally prove rewarding to the operator, but we must never make the mistake of assuming that all operators will perform according to some statistical law, or some other assumption by the system designer. As we have seen, there may be reasons (good and evil) why the operator doesn't *want* to work more efficiently, and these may have to be overcome through external motivation rather than system design. (See, for example, Gilb, 1973, Chapter 4, Motivational Tactics.)

DEFINING "EFFICIENCY"

Alternatively, we may simply have to or want to accept the operator's decision about how efficiently to operate. Consider a hospital information system in which doctors enter dosage quantities for various drugs. While we may provide default dosages, we will probably not want to make any great effort to force the doctors to change their habits in writing prescriptions--though we may want to provide feedback which they may use at *their* option.

In the cases of doctors, total usage of the system may not justify attempting to gain efficiency, though other operators of the same system may be justified in striving for speed of entry. Even then, however, we simply cannot know what will be most efficient for each and every *individual* person.

For instance, in one system with default quantities for each line item, some of the operators simply would not use default quantities at all. Others would use them, but only for quantities of "one." Since some of these operators were actually faster overall than some who used defaults consistently, it was decided that there was no need to try to make people break their own "rhythm." We don't know, of course, whether or not these operators could indeed have gone faster by taking fuller advantage of defaults, but chances are they knew themselves fairly well.

DESIGNING FOR INDIVIDUAL VARIATION

Because people are different, and situations are different, it is wise to allow for differences rather than fight them. Feedback, for instance, allows people to learn at their own rate and in their own manner, unlike classroom instruction where all must cover the same material at the same speed, whether they learn it or not.

EQUIVALENCE OF DEFAULT FORMS

On the other hand, if learning is to be a genuine possibility, then the various alternative means of expression should be related in a "rational" way. Thus, the full explicit version:

JONC AIR 6 JG4889 1 JG338

should have *exactly* the same meaning as its various default forms, such as

JONC 6 JG4889 1 JG338

JONC 6 JG4889 JG338

JONC AIR JG4889 1 JG338

JONC JG4889 JG338

Ensuring this equivalence requires careful input design and systematic programming methods. The input designer must work out and review all possible variations of the input defaults. Here is a checklist of considerations:

Write out all expected variations.

If the total number of variations is too large, make use of a formal grammar of some kind. (The one used in Weinberg (1970) is quite easily used

for input design problems, and will be used in this book where necessary.) The formal grammar can be used as an object for studying the system and testing its variations, or as a design tool to reduce the complexity of the input situation.

Write out examples of variations that can occur through errors of various kinds.

If the number of variations is too large, work as in the second step to reduce the apparent complexity.

Make sure each expected variation results in a uniquely interpretable meaning for all planned data, or data which might be included in later extensions. (See Wilcox, in press, for a discussion of ambiguous grammars.)

Specify the action *to be taken by the program in each of the error variations. These could be "error, try again" messages or reasonable default options, with some kind of logging for statistical purposes.*

TESTING FOR EQUIVALENCE

The programmer, on the other hand, must not *expect* the designer to have thoroughly explored all possible combinations. The programmer should therefore feel responsible for finding additional variations which must be considered and for ensuring that the program can handle these variations in a reasonable manner-- consistent with the original design specifications.

Sets of test cases should be created in some systematic manner. Formal grammatical descriptions will greatly aid here, and may even allow a table-driven program structure which will be easily tested.

In any case, systematic test cases should *always* be supplemented with:

some "random" data

some live human data, generated by people who

know nothing about the internal system structure

Some "absolute garbage" data, perhaps generated by searching wastebaskets for cards, or turning input cards upside down.

Proper feedback, built into the program and related to the input formats in a rational way, will help ensure that no errors of programming or operator interpretation work their way very far into the system's defenses.

PHASING IN DEFAULTS

There may be hardware reasons for providing explicit forms of the default options. In a system with several types of data entry equipment, some of the equipment may not have the necessary computing power to fill in the defaults, or to provide feedback. In such instances, it may not be a good design to let the whole system suffer by limiting your input design to techniques which can be used by *all* of the mixed hardware devices. The system strength should not be limited by the weakest link in the chain, but should be based on the best results from the available mix of devices.

Stations which have the necessary power can provide the defaults, but should also provide the explicit form so that there is operator compatibility with the less powerful stations. If and when the limited stations are upgraded for full capability, the changeover can be made without explicit training. The feedback itself can gradually and naturally bring the advantages of more efficient operation to the old operators.

ESTABLISHING THE DEFAULTS

The first problem in establishing defaults is whether to do it at all. Roughly speaking, if fewer than 1/3 of all cases will default, there may not be sufficient practice for the operators to learn the system. A sample of the present inputs can help determine if this level has been reached, or can be reached by re-structuring.

MULTI-LEVEL DEFAULTS

If the input sample doesn't show any obvious default, there may still be opportunities for "multi-level" defaults. For example, in the input sample we might find the following distribution of order quantities:

Quantity	Frequency
1	25%
2	20%
3	15%
4	10%
10	10%
12	10%

with all other order quantities making up the other 10%. A default order quantity of 1 might be all right, but the high frequency of other quantities suggests there might be some deeper structure.

It might be, for example, that *certain products* had characteristic order quantities, as we have seen. In that case 6 different product categories might be established, according to typical quantity ordered.

Another possiblility for hidden structures might be the ordering pattern of certain buyers. Instead of product categories, we might want to establish *customer categories*, with a default for each customer. The operators, however, could not be expected to memorize all customers' categories, so at the beginning of each order, the terminal could inform the operator of that customer's defaults. Or, the operator could scan the order list and establish a default that would be convenient for that particular order.

AUTOMATIC ESTABLISHMENT OF DEFAULTS

With operators setting defaults for each other, we come close to a more flexible method of establishing defaults. The system itself could tabulate patterns of input--for each product, or each customer, or for some other category. For example, if one customer generally orders one category of item, such as "SCREWS," the system can "announce" that default as soon as the customer information has been keyed and confirmed.

Automatic adaptive setting of defaults can have several advantages:

Defaults may be used in situations where the raw frequency was not sufficiently high.

No great initial expense is needed to establish defaults, for they establish themselves automatically.

When patterns change, defaults will gradually change to meet those new patterns, without explicit intervention.

Pattern information obtained in this system may prove useful for understanding system behavior such as buying patterns of customers.

PROTECTION AGAINST HARMFUL DEFAULTS

In deciding when to use defaults, and what default values to use, we must consider the consequences of inadvertently getting the default option because of an input error. Although proper feedback can reduce such errors substantially, there is no reason to assume that an operator will always be paying full attention to the video unit.

As a case in point, consider the prescription of drugs in the hospital information system. A certain drug is used in two distinct disease situations--one requiring a dosage of 500 milligrams and the other, 50 milligrams. If, by some error, a 50-milligram

patient is fed a 500-milligram dose, he is likely to
be "cured" once and for all of his worldly woes.   In
this situation, even though the 500-milligram dose is
used for 98% of the prescriptions, it will be appropriate to use 50 milligrams as the default, or to have
no default at all.

DESIGN OF DEFAULT OR BY DEFAULT?

Other situations may not be so serious as this,
but the principle is clear--default errors can occur
and must be weighed in the design.   The choice among
evils may not be easy, but will always be better than
not facing up to the difficulties at all.   As we shall
see later, there are a variety of other design techniques that could be used to fortify the default design.   In the hospital situation, for instance, we
could improve control if a statement of disease type
was available to the input routines, to check against
the prescribed dosage.   But whatever approach we take,
we shouldn't leave our *design* decisions to "default,"
or Murphy's Law will surely bring us to our knees.

A SUMMARY OF EXPECTED ATTRIBUTES

The following is a simplified multidimensional view
of the normal attributes which the designer can expect
when specifying the default technique.   The designer
must calculate or otherwise estimate the more accurate
attributes for his particular implementation in order
to compare this option against other design alternatives.

PRODUCTIVITY:

The keying effort is reduced by a predictable,
simply-calculated amount, or an amount that increases
over time with operator learning and motivation.

RELIABILITY:

Default options, since they are programmed, are rarely subject to human error. Normally, a default option should be *acceptable* as a worst case occurence in case it is exercised by accident.

PORTABILITY:

The default option can be transported to all kinds of data recording equipment with little or no change. Some feedback options, however, become counterproductive if the transfer is from electronic display to mechanical printing or even off-line. Also, the default values themselves may have to be modified if the system is used under different conditions, as in a different branch of the same store, or in the wholesale operations instead of the retail.

IMPLEMENTATION EASE:

Analysis, design, and programming efforts may be increased though efforts may actually be reduced if feedback is employed. Moreover, if properly designed, the naturalness of the system should reduce cutover costs from previous systems, including operator training and the costs of early errors.

HARDWARE RESOURCES:

A few additional lines of code per default option will probably suffice. Extensive use of defaults could result in an unacceptable hardware burden in some environments with limited resources, such as "intelligent" but not "brilliant" data collection devices. Insertion of defaults in such situations could be done by a more central CPU, at the designer's option.

SECURITY:

Default options (without feedback, of course) can give security against interception since messages may not be interpretable without knowledge of the defaults.

EXTENDABILITY:

Default options are potentially dangerous when extending the input message with new elements, since ambiguities are easily introduced. Any extension should be considered with the care and precautions of a new design, with respect to both ambiguity and error-proneness.

DESIGN EXERCISES:

1. Design (or redesign) a simplified version of an input system which you are currently using, or is of future interest. Examples of input and other details should be simplified enough to fit on a single page without crowding. Answer the following questions as well as you can:

a. By how much is the keying effort reduced compared with the previous design, or designs of colleagues?

b. By how much is the machine processing time reduced (or increased) for 1000 input lines?

c. Will your design be applicable to all types of input devices, such as telex, card punch, display terminal, key to cassette? If not, what variants would make it applicable, and at what conversion cost?

d. Estimate the error rate of your design, and compare it with error rates of other designs for the system.

e. Estimate the programming effort (in lines of code in your programming language, and in programmer hours and test duration) needed to support your design.

f.   Estimate the real and secondary (virtual or
overlay) space needed to implement your program.
What percentage of the code can be resident on
secondary storage without affecting performance
of this part of the logic by more than 5%?

g.   Specify at least 10 recognizable input error
conditions and their error handling to maximize
human productivity at a given level of error
reaching the next stage of the system.

h.   Specify, if possible, the formal grammar for
the input transaction, and show how it can be
used in implementing the program and/or the test
cases.

2.   In an operating system, the designers are choosing
defaults for the job control language. When a new
data set (file) is written on a direct access device,
and no disposition is specified, there is a choice of
defaults:

a.   The data set could be *deleted* by default, so
as to protect against unwarranted accumulation
of unwanted data sets that somebody forgot to
delete explicitly.

b.   The data set could be *saved* by default, so
as to protect against wasting an important run
just because somebody forgot to save explicitly.

c.   The saving and deleting of the data set could
be made to depend on other factors such as its
size, naming conventions, currently available
space, or user characteristics, such as priority
or security classification.

d.   No defaults at all could be allowed. Discuss
the tradeoffs among these design alternatives.
Indicate at least one situation in which each of
them would be the preferred design.

3.   In an order entry system, each order consists
primarily of a long list of quantities and product

codes.   If each product code is 3 characters long,
and if a default quantity of "one" is used, show how
the amount of keying depends on the frequency of "one"
orders, assuming the default is used whenever possible.
Produce an equation or graph displaying this sensitivity.   Describe how this behavior is related to error
behavior in this application.

4.   Derive a formal grammatical description of the
system of input shown in the text with such entries as

    JONC 6 JG4889 1 JG338

    JONC AIR JG4889 1 JG338

starting with the definition of an entry:

    <u>entry</u>---<u>customer-code</u>   <u>shipping-method</u>   <u>line-item</u>

Using your grammar, show how the entry

    JONCO LAND JG338

could be ambiguous if there is a product code LAND.
Discuss what the designer and/or programmer could do
about such an ambiguity.   Write down a minimal set of
test cases, based on the grammar, and show the full
interpretation of each correct case.   Write down the
three most likely errors, and describe how the system
ought to handle them.

Chapter III

Positional Messages

Just the place for a Snark!

--The Hunting of the Snark, Fit the First

As the bellman knew, every Snark has its place, though
there may not be a Snark in every place. Thinking in
terms of *where* a thing belongs is quite natural to us,
be we Bellmen, Boots, Bonnet-makers, Barristers, Brok-
ers, Billiard-makers, Bankers, Bakers, Butchers, or
Brilliant Designers. By placing data elements in appropriate positional relationships, we can often a-
chieve naturalness of entry, elimination of redundancy,
and control of error--as we now shall see.

TECHNIQUES

Positional messages are interpreted on the basis of
the location of individual data elements. This location may be in relation to reference points, or in
relation to other data elements in the message.

VARIABLE-LENGTH ITEMS

Consider the problem of entering a list of words. Using fixed-field format, each field will have to allow for the longest possible word, as in

ADDER   DISCRIMINATOR   ROTOR

If the field size is 20, 60 characters will be needed for these three words. Problems of alignment may be minimized by tabulation or skipping, but we still might have to store and transmit 60 characters. In addition, reading is difficult.

Consider the same three words using a positional message:

ADDER DISCRIMINATOR ROTOR

Only 26 characters are needed instead of 60, and read-ability is improved. There are 23 characters for the words themselves, and 3 for the blanks to delimit the words.

VARIABLE-LENGTH LISTS

Consider a student registration application, in which each student chooses a list of courses for the semester. Some students take a single course; others take as many as 7. With fixed fields, all student entries must explicitly fill the 7 fields. With proper equipment, we can use a tab or skip per field, as in

ANT1¢ ENG12¢   ¢   ¢   ¢   ¢   ¢

If the course list is the *last* thing on the input message, we may be able to skip out the entire message with a single keystroke, as in

ANT1¢ ENG12¢

where "¢" stands for "finish the line" or "feed the next line or card."

Another approach to reducing the tabbing is to require the course numbers to be fixed lengths, so that individual fields need not be marked with tab positions. In that case, the above example would be keyed as

ANT001ENG012¢

This approach requires

thousands of students to learn to write leading zeros, contrary to their natural inclination

extra strokes within each field that would otherwise be shorter

maximum field size to be fixed at all times

In the tab approach, the operator has to make extra keystrokes and also *count the fields*. The line feed method solves these problems but locks us into an inflexible format, in case we ever want to add a new message element at the end of the course list field. Moreover, the line feed method can be used for only one list per line.

Positional data can solve each of these problems. The above example in a positional system could be keyed as

ANT1 ENG12

which is

easier to read

easier to key, with fewer strokes and no counting

readily expandable, either in number of items, size of items, or other lists

more natural for the thousands of people specifying course selections

To be sure, many of us are now so accustomed to form-filling that we meekly submit to filling in leading zeros, lettering within boxes, and all the other insults poor input design has forced upon us. As we will see, however, our sheepish acceptance is usually accompanied by an unconscious desire to undermine the system. This desire is ultimately reflected in input errors--errors not readily detected or corrected by rigid input systems.

For instance, positional listing of the courses frees us from fixing the field length, so we could easily expand the system to allow such variations as

ANTHRO1 ENGL12

ANTHRO-1 ENGL-12

which are much less likely to be confused with

ANAT-1 ENGIN-12

But *you* knew that ENG stood for "ENGLISH," didn't you?

DELIMITERS

Because positional items are in *relative* positions, explicit symbols or keystrokes may be needed to delimit:

the start of a list

the end of a list

the start of one list item

the end of one list item

Such delimiters add to the total keying required to enter a list, but this overhead is commonly reduced in several ways.

For instance, the start-list delimiter is ordinarily implicit, as when the list starts:

at the beginning of a message

at the beginning of a particular line of the message

at the end of some fixed-field in the message.

Similarly, the end-list delimiter may be implicit, as when the list ends:

with the end of the message

with the end of a particular line of the message

at the beginning of some fixed field in the message.

at the end of some fixed number of list items

The delimiters *between* items are ordinarily combined into a single delimiter that ends one item and begins the next. In the list

ADDER DISCRIMINATOR ROTOR

the *blank* achieves the two delimiting functions. The delimiter must not be a character that might be found in the items themselves, which sometimes restricts the choice. For instance, if some words in the above application are composite, the blank as delimiter would create ambiguities, as in

CONTROL RELAY LINE SWITCH SERVO

Typically, a comma or semicolon is used instead of a blank. For instance:

CONTROL RELAY,LINE SWITCH,SERVO

which completely resolves the ambiguity.

Sometimes, "extra" blanks are added for readability:

CONTROL RELAY, LINE SWITCH, SERVO

In this case, the blank before each item *could* be considered the start-item delimiter. This choice, however, removes some flexibility, as we see in this version:

CONTROL RELAY,   LINE SWITCH,SERVO

This list could lead to such erroneous entries as "ØØLINEØSWITCH"--or to complete chaos over the "missing" blank before SERVO. A much more human interpretation allows liberal use of blanks, in keeping with natural interpretations.

THE BLANK

In the design of the Job Control Language (JCL) for the IBM/360 Operating System, a blank was used to delimit the start of a variable-length comment field in a control card. Thus, for instance, in the card

        //WMASTER DD DCB=(LRECL=80, RECFM=FB, BLKSIZE=800,

the blank after the comma (LRECL=80,β...) rendered the remainder of the card inoperative. This convention was so unnatural that *thousands* of JCL errors were made, and are still made, on its account. We could *conservatively* estimate that this poor choice of a blank delimiter cost IBM customers around the world over $100,000,000 in reruns, destroyed files, inefficient operation, and bug hunting.

The "natural" interpretation of a blank buried in text is quite different. Blanks generally follow these rules in natural text:

> *Two blanks have the same significance as one blank.*
>
> *A blank before or after another delimiter is not significant as a delimiter itself.*
>
> *A blank not next to any other delimiter is significant in itself.*

A subroutine to apply these rules will properly interpret the list:

        CONTROL RELAY,   LINE SWITCH ,SERVO

and will make data entry far more reliable--especially in applications using "typists" instead of "punchers."

THE POSITIONING COMMA

Another costly delimiter design mistake was also built into the IBM OS/360 JCL--this one worth perhaps $50,000,000. An example occurs in the SPACE parameter in JCL. One list in the SPACE parameter contained up to three items, which might look like this:

        (100,20,5)

If, however, the middle item was *missing*, you were supposed to write:

        (100,,5)

The "extra," or "positioning" comma told the system that you didn't mean:

(100,5)

Of course, you weren't supposed to put a *blank* between those commas, on pain of costly punishment. The whole approach was so unnatural that beginning users had no more than a 10% chance of getting it right the first time--and experienced users didn't do much better, especially when they had to write such monstrosities as

SPACE=(50,(50,,5),,,ROUND)

The problem with the positioning comma, like with the "extra" blank, is that it goes against the grain of ordinary usage. The list *looks* reasonably natural-- so we are more easily tricked when naturalness is violated.

But what can we do when there are missing elements? One thing we could *try* is to *document* the deviations from naturalness. Robert Horn (1975) gives the following example describing how to handle the missing information problem:

> Occasionally, there will be a series of measurements which, for one reason or another, have missing values....You can indicate a not-present value in the INPUT statement by *not* placing a value between two commas or semicolons....
> *You type:*
> INPUT MEAS: .01, .09,   , 2.4, 3.4, 7.9, 8.2, 9.3
> Note that two commas occur in a row in the place where the value is not present in the data...

This helpful documentation is supplemented by two arrows pointing to the place where the double comma is found. Of course, the arrows--and large parts of the "excellent" documentation--would not be necessary if a different input design were used.

DESIGN AS A SUBSTITUTE FOR DOCUMENTATION

Without further explanation, we can document an

alternative design in the following way:

> Occasionally, there will be a series of measure-
> ments which, for one reason or another, have
> missing values. You indicate missing values in
> this way:
> INPUT MEAS: .01, .09, ?, 2.4, 3.4, 7.9, 8.2, 9.3

The moral here is simple:

> ### DON'T TRY TO CORRECT POOR DESIGN
> ### WITH GOOD DOCUMENTATION

If a system *seems* reasonably natural, no amount
of documentation will overcome the effect of unnatural
exceptions. If it could, the millions spent by IBM
would surely have overcome the JCL problems of significant blanks and positioning commas.

Instead of using documentation as a *solution* to
poor design, we should use it as a *symptom* of poor
design. The more documentation we need, the poorer
the design. And the more documentation to read, the
fewer the readers.

Instead of documenting a solution, we should seek
a solution that will document itself. In this case,
the solution will be instantly recognized by the users
as the "natural" way to specify missing items:

> If the item is missing, use a question mark (?)
> in its place.

This solution shows a feeling for human psychology,
the one instinct every input designer must have.

JUSTIFICATION

Positional data can be justified in a design for reasons of naturalness, efficiency, or both at once.

NATURALNESS

The basis for the naturalness of positional messages is "sequential memory," which all human beings
possess. We may not recall a melody, but if the first

bar is played for us, we quickly hum the rest.

To feel your sequential memory at work, try to recall the *middle* line of a familiar song, rhyme, or speech. This kind of random recall is almost impossible--unless you start with the first few words, as in:

> Oh, say can you...
>
> Mary had a little...
>
> Fourscore and seven...

In other words, for sequential memory to operate, we need a *synchronization point*. Many different techniques are available to get us started. The "first" element is only one of several possibilities--one that too often carries over from the days of fixed-field positional systems.

EFFICIENCY OF VARIABLE ITEMS

Quantitatively, positional data is justified on two counts:

> *saving strokes because of shortened fields-- i.e., no field filling*
>
> *saving strokes because of omitted fields-- i.e., defaults*

In machine terms, effective transmission capacity may be reduced far more than keystrokes, especially if variation in field size is great. In human terms, errors may be similarly reduced.

For instance, consider the example of entering a word list. In a fixed-field approach, the critical parameters will be the number of words and the *length of the longest word*, since that length will have to be allowed for *every* word. In one application, the longest "word" known with certainty was

ELECTRONIC POTENTIOMETER PYROMETER

or 34 characters. Because cards were punched from various catalogs, nobody was *sure* this was the longest. Therefore, the designers were prepared to allow 40 characters--two words per card. To punch 50,000 words,

25,000 cards would be required--2,000,000 characters that would have to be transmitted or read.

Using a variable-field approach, the critical parameters were number of words and *average length of a word*. In this case, the *average* length was no greater than 9 characters--plus one character to be allowed for the delimiter, a comma. Using this appr-oach, only about 1/4 the number of cards and charact-ers were needed.

EFFICIENCY OF VARIABLE LISTS

There are two distinct methods of handling lists with missing items:

padding the list with "missing item symbols" so that the number of items in the list appears constant

using defaults so that missing items need not be specified at all

The first method simplifies programming at the expense of data entry problems. The second method may require slightly more programming, but usually results in an improved keying environment.

The most common method of implementing defaults is by arranging the items in *frequency order*. That is, the most frequent item comes first in the list, the next most frequent second, and so forth. This order is naturally achieved when the list merely con-tains a variable number of coequal items, as in our student registration example. There, the critical factors are *average item length* and *average list length*.

Frequency ordering simplifies keying by reducing the average list length. Consider the following ex-ample from a labor distribution application. There are four items of information to be entered, as shown in Figure 3.1.

The most common case is an employee working ex-actly 8 hours in his or her regularly assigned depart-ment. In that case, the default entry is simply the

Item	Format	Frequency	Default
Employee identifier	2–4 digits	100%	none
Department charged	3–6 characters	30%	"home" department
Regular hours	number with up to one decimal place and two other digits	15%	8
Premium hours	same as regular hours	5%	0

Figure 3.1   Four items used in a labor
distribution application.

employee number by itself. By placing the fields in
the order of decreasing frequency, we get the following types of entries and their frequencies:

TYPICAL ENTRY	FREQUENCY	AVERAGE LENGTH
117	70%	4
129,ASSEM	15%	10
94,INSPEC,3.5	10%	14
188,SHIP,8,2.3	5%	18

Because field lengths vary, we must have average field
length to compute average message length. Based on
the averages given above, the weighted average of
overall keystrokes is 6.6 per entry. This compares
favorably with 8.9 strokes for a fixed-field approach,
with field skipping.

Errors will probably be reduced more than keystrokes, for one or more of the following reasons:

*No counting of fields, or of positions within a
field, is needed.*

*Form-filling is reduced, or eliminated, depending
on the actual source.*

> *More tolerance of variation is permitted, such as 0129 or 129 for employee number, 4 or 4.0 for hours worked.*

Total cost savings could be 2/1, 3/1, or even higher.

NON-TRAILING POSITIONAL DATA

In the days when the only input media were punch cards and paper tapes, *trailing* data was the only "natural" positional form. In those days, processing and memory were expensive, and backspacing a card deck or paper tape was generally impossible. The ideal input design permitted a program to examine each input element without consideration of the trailing elements. No memory was required, and processing was simplicity itself. The strain on the user was not considered unimportant--it was simply not considered at all.

CONTENT DEPENDENCY

From the human point of view, however, there are other positional situations that may be superior to the simple trailing scheme. For instance, suppose we were keying telephone numbers (USA system) which consisted of a list of three parts--area code, exchange, and number, as in

    402 781 2368

    402 436 1212

We observe that most of the phone numbers (95%) used by this local business are in the same area code (402), and that of these, 45% are in the same (downtown) exchange (436). If we were using a trailing positional list for the telephone number, we could key the above numbers in shorter forms as

    2368 781   *(402 is the default area code)*

    1212   *(436 is the default exchange)*

Although this approach would certainly decrease raw keying effort, we can be almost certain that it will induce many errors. Why? Because of the tremendous power of the "natural" order of telephone numbers: area code, exchange, and *then* number.

Our outmoded thinking patterns make us ignore the obvious solution to such problems--a non-trailing positional list. Let the operators key the telephone numbers in a "natural" order, but let the computer make sense out of default cases. When the program receives 781, it may not immediately know whether this is an area code or an exchange. (In the USA, it *could* know by other means.) Once the remainder of the list is available in memory, however, the program will have no difficulty recognizing the difference between:

781 2368 *and* 781 495 3477

In other words, the computer determines the identity of each element not by *fixed* relative position, but in the context of the *entire* list. Another excellent example is the "natural" order of people's names:

ELIZABETH RUTH LESSMAN

JIM BOB O'LINCOLN

Typically, when names are given as variable-list items, sorting convenience dictates the annoying "last name first" rule that is so contrary to the average American's or European's culture. Moreover, if anything is missing from a name, it is likely to be the *middle* name, and after that, the first name. Frequency ordering therefore dictates the "last name first" rule.

Several generations of Americans and Europeans have borne this insult to their very names. In the United States, those without middle names have often had to accept the further indignity of taking "NMI" (for "no middle initial") as a middle name, just so the preallocated field could be filled with *something*. No wonder people doubt who is in control, people or machines.

NATURAL NAMING

The public image of computers would improve immediately if natural naming could be adopted. One census *started* with the objective of natural naming. They considered combinations such as the following, which might be ambiguous by the names alone:

GEORGE ALLEN MICHAEL

MICHAEL ALLEN

GEORGE

The first is entirely clear, being of the conventional form:

first-name   middle-name   last-name
GEORGE   ALLEN   MICHAEL

The second is also clear, since the middle name is most often omitted:

first-name   last-name
MICHAEL   ALLEN

Only the third case might give us trouble, for we often call our friends by their first name only. The computer, however, is nobody's friend (or everybody's) so we can assume with confidence that when a single name is given, it has to be the *last* name.

The three forms of name in this application are:

first-name middle-name last-name

first-name last-name

last-name

The program to interpret these names works as follows:

1. Read the entire list of 1, 2, or 3 elements into memory.

2. If there is a single element, it is a last name.

3. If there are two elements, they are first name and last name.

4. If there are three elements, they are first name, middle name, and last name.

Thus, the meaning of a particular element does depend on its *position* in the set, but the *way* it depends on position depends on the *number* of elements in the set.

This positional design proved to be perfectly natural for the census-takers, with no training required. Inasmuch as 40% of the cases had a last name only and 40% had two names only, the average name set had 1.8 names--precisely the reduction expected from a trailing positional system, but with many fewer name-reversal errors.

An order of magnitude gain was registered in both reliability and user comfort--at the cost of a moderate increase in programming difficulty and computer time.

COPING WITH RARE EXCEPTIONS

The natural name system, when put into practice, had one flaw. From time to time, partial information concerning people already in the census came in *after* the original entry. Although this partial information affected the names in fewer than 1% of the cases, there were instances in which a first name only, or a middle name only, or a first name and a middle name only, were to be added to an existing record.

Because the meaning of the entered names was determined by the position in the entire set of names, it was impossible to enter a single first name without having it interpreted as a last name. For a short time, the designers feared that the entire system would have to be discarded in favor of a more clumsy but complete approach.

We must not let one exceptional case destroy an otherwise attractive message design. Usually, we can find a simple way to handle the exception, without doing dirt to our overall scheme. That's one of the principal advantages of computers (or should be)--we can afford to handle exceptions exceptionally if we get a benefit greater than the cost.

In case after case, this approach has paid off. We certainly appreciate a simple system with no exceptions or deviations. Yet, we must not penalize the mass of transactions for the benefit of an elite rare or improbable data combination.

A useful design principle, therefore, is this:
DESIGN FOR THE MASSES, THEN DESIGN THE EXCEPTION LOGIC.

EXCEPTION DESIGNS

In the case at hand, the natural name patterns handled the masses, but how could exceptions be handled without disturbing this pattern? We know that extra documentation won't work. Perhaps we can create a conventional symbol that will signal an exceptional case. We could, for instance, let the *asterisk* stand for

"...and use the *existing* name for *this* position."

In this approach, the message

GEORGE *

would be read as

Change the first name to GEORGE
and use the existing last name.

The asterisk acts as a place marker for the last name, so the computer knows by the count of 2 that GEORGE is a first name. In a similar way, the computer and the people will naturally give the same interpretation to these cases:

GEORGE * *   *Change the first name to*
                  GEORGE--this is a redundant
                  but perfectly correct varia-
                  tion of GEORGE *

* GEORGE *   *Change the middle name to*
                  GEORGE

GEORGE ALLEN *   *Change the first name to*
                  GEORGE and the middle name
                  to ALLEN

Another approach, if the original information is present or available to the operator through inquiry, is to *rekey* the existing data. Because the percentage of such cases is small, the total keying effort would not be greatly increased, but rekeying could increase the probability of error. Feedback comparison between old and new names could help control such rekeying errors.

Possibly the best approach combines the special "existing name" symbol with feedback to ensure correct interpretation in potentially confusing cases. For example, consider the following dialogue:

GEORGE *

NEW NAME IS GEORGE MICHAEL

OLD NAME WAS STEVEN MICHAEL

At this point, the operator recognizes a mistake, for the intention was to enter GEORGE as the *middle* name. The dialogue thus continues somewhat like this:

STEVEN GEORGE *

NEW NAME IS STEVEN GEORGE MICHAEL

OLD NAME WAS GEORGE MICHAEL

RESYNCHRONIZATION

A very common sort of positional interpretation of messages is suggested by this example:

IGNORE THIS LINE BECAUSE OF DASHES AT END----

In this case, the "----" at the "end" of the message is an error signal that obeys the following rule:

Four (or more) consecutive dashes at the extreme right end of the text of the message line shall result in that line being deleted.

A useful variant of this idea is indicated by another example:

I SAW THIS WAS WRONG AFTER THE END OF THE LINE

The series of dashes standing alone is a signal to delete the immediately preceding line. Such correction is particularly useful for sequential recording media such as paper tape or cassette tape.

PARTIAL CORRECTION

If we are willing to forgo the use of some symbol string *within* any message (and not just at the end), we can use the same approach for partial correction, or *resynchronization*, of a message. For instance, if we are not otherwise using the slash (/) character, we can assign to it the meaning:

"Delete *one* preceding item."

The following corrections are then possible:

ORIGINAL	EQUIVALENT TO
12 23 102 / 103	12 23 103
10 WTR 97.5 // RDR 38	10 RDR 38
2 MMY / MTR 88 / 20	2 MTR 20

For reliable operation, the system should echo the actual message as received in cases where corrections are attempted, as in the dialogue:

2 MMY / MTR 88 // 20

INPUT IS: 2   20

2 MMY 20 // MTR 20

INPUT IS: 2   MTR   20

Resynchronization on an element-by-element basis is particularly useful when:

The operator may be unskilled.

The positional list is long, so that it is unlikely that the operator can complete an error-free sequence.

FINITE-STATE DESCRIPTIONS

What we call "resynchronization" relates directly to what automata theorists call "state reset." (see Florentin and Sammes, 1975.) In designing positional input systems, particularly with such features as re-synchronization, it is helpful to employ the description methods for finite automata. (see, for example, Minsky, 1967.) For instance, the method used in the previous example could be sketched as shown in Figure 3.2, or in some equivalent form.

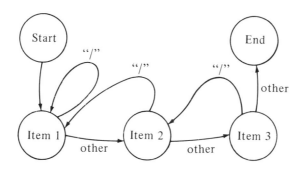

Figure 3.2   A finite-state transition diagram showing resynchronization, or state-reset.

Each node in the figure represents a state of the input process, and each directed line represents a transition from one state to another. At the start of the line, we are in the START state. From there, the first input "item" will send us to the state ITEM1. If there are no error corrections, the states will progress through the sequence:

START   ITEM1   ITEM2   ITEM3   END

which confirms the "normal" case.

Any slash following an item sends the state back to the previous item, thus cancelling the previous item. The cancellation is probably implemented by removing the top element from a push-down stack.

The state-transition diagram helps us to visualize the consequences of various input behaviors, and also serves as a model for an input program. Indeed,

many input systems--and particularly positional ones--
can be implemented most easily using a table-driven
finite-state machine. The tables for the "machine"
can be written directly from the state-transition
diagram, so that a single program can handle any number of different input systems, merely by changing
tables. (See, for example, Weinberg, Yasukawa, and
Marcus, 1973, Section 8.3.)

OVERSTRIKING

In many terminal systems, the *backspace* character
is used to permit character-by-character resynchronization. This device is frequently used for the entry
of computer programs, in which the previous "item" may
be difficult to determine.

The backspace technique has its dangers, though,
for it is difficult to determine--looking at a listing
of the interaction--what actually entered the computer.
You can see this difficulty if you try to interpret
such a line as:

350 ABC

Even if you can make out the overstruck characters, you have no way of knowing which was struck first.
Was the first part 350 overstruck with 7, or 357 overstruck with 0? As for the second part, which is ABC
overstruck with XYZ, there are 8 different combinations that give this constellation--if you don't count
different backspacing patterns as different.

When using a system of backspace and overstrike,
we should always provide for echoing the actual input,
as in the dialogue:

350 ABC

INPUT IS: 357XBZ

When a message uses no overstriking, the echo can be
omitted. Of course, if a video unit with backspace-
erase is used, the echo appears naturally in all
cases for sight verification.

RECORDING OF ERRORS

It's always dangerous to leave no record of what was done. A *minimal* requirement for any error-correcting system is an error-log. The log's job is to ensure that every error is recorded--on tape, or disk, or some other processing medium.

Once the log exists, other programs can generate reports that show patterns in the errors. If there is a design flaw that induces errors, it may produce a recognizable pattern on one of these reports. For instance, we see below a portion of a report obtained by sorting error records from the log and tabulating them into categories:

ITEM NAME:		TRANSACTION CODE	
DESCRIPTION:		ALPHA, POSITIONAL, VARYING	
TOTAL ENTRIES COVERED BY LOG = 37,412			
REPORTING THRESHOLD FOR ANY ERROR = 5			
CORRECT CODE	KEYED AS	CORRECTION PATTERN	FREQUENCY IN SAMPLE
RFE	REF	--FE	196
RFE	REF	--EF--FE	14

This portion of the report reveals a strong tendency to key RFE as REF. The tendency is so strong that in 14 cases, the same error was made on the first attempt at correction. ("--EF--FE" means "backspace, backspace, E, F, backspace, backspace, F, E".)

What should be done with such information? One possibility is to ignore it, under the assumption that the operators are catching the error themselves. This assumption, however, fails to take several important factors into account:

For each such error the operator catches, there may be one or more not caught until later, when correction is far more costly.

Even correctable errors slow operations or annoy the operator.

Breaking the pace of error-free entry may induce further errors--errors which may not be correctable.

Another possibility is to change the code to REF, which the operators seem to favor. In that case, however, we might find even more errors in the other direction. A better possibility is to *tolerate variation* and accept *both* RFE and REF as correct. We will have much more to say about this approach in a later chapter.

Whatever approach we take should be better than no approach at all. If we hadn't tabulated the error log, we might never have known there was a problem to solve. This kind of head-in-the-sand ignorance may be all right for ostriches, but input designers had better memorize this rule:

NEVER ALLOW AN ERROR CORRECTION TO GO UNRECORDED.

DESIGN FOR RELIABILITY

One great advantage of positional messages is low redundancy. Properly designed positional messages may approach the theoretical minimum keystrokes needed to enter the information. Yet, as with most good things, there is another side to the coin. The other side of the minimum redundancy coin is reliability.

THREE-STAGE DESIGN

The most difficult error to detect in positional messages is a *misordering* of items. The problem is similar to putting fixed-field items in the wrong fields. How is the computer to know that when you keyed

CHESTER ARTHUR

you *meant* to key

ARTHUR CHESTER

instead? There isn't enough information in these items *by themselves* to make a correction, or even detect an error. If detection is to be possible, it must be based on relationships with other information in the message or in some stored data.

The first step, however, is to work on ways of *minimizing* the errors, rather than patching them up after the fact. We can protect ourselves against error-prone designs by employing a three-stage design procedure:

a. *Select "natural" sequences to reduce errors.*

b. *Specify error recognition, handling, and recording.*

c. *If (b) proves too difficult, redesign the codes, adding redundancy to make them distinguishable from other codes in the sequence.*

HOW MANY ITEMS IN SEQUENCE?

Choices made in step (a) of the design process may lay a heavy hand on step (b). A skeptical analysis of all possible error situations grows most difficult as the *number* of items in sequence grows. By reducing the number of items, we sharply reduce the number of error permutations to be considered.

With two items, there is but one erroneous sequence. With three items, there are five. With four, twenty-three. If some items may be omitted, the number of error possibilities is even higher. This rapid growth suggests a limiting factor on the positional technique, unless the sequence is so natural that error probabilities are low.

LONGER LISTS

As with any rule of thumb, there are exceptions to the limit of 3 or 4 items in a positional list. A significant exception is a list for which either:

no order need be applied, or

ordering can be done in the program, rather than before entry.

As an example of the first situation--no order needed--consider the entry of responses by different respondents to a single question in a survey. Because the respondents are not individually identified, no particular importance is attached to the precise order of entry. Lists of ten or more items can thus be used with impunity. What is important in such an unsequenced application is the integrity of the individual items. Therefore, some kind of checking should be incorporated to count the items and verify the count against a control.

As an example of the second situation--ordering done by the program--consider the following system designed for entry of pharmacological information in a hospital information system. A physician would write a list of medications for a particular patient, along with dosage and frequency information. One line item on the list might look like this:

ALLOPURINOL 50MG   4/DAY

After these entries were keyed, they were checked against a stored list of available drugs. For programming convenience, however, all drugs for one patient had to be done in alphabetical order before checking could be done. A list such as

ASPIRIN 2 4/DAY ALLOPURINOL 50MG 4/DAY

would be rejected, because ASPIRIN and ALLOPURINOL are not in alphabetical order!

The physicians were *supposed* to write the items in order, but nobody could force them to do it. Even when the physicians tried, they made errors. Therefore, the keying operators were told to scan the list and key items in alphabetical order. Naturally, they went very slowly and made numerous errors.

Here, obviously, the job of sorting should have been done by the computer, but the programmer was afraid to "touch the program." In view of the risk to patients given wrong prescriptions, the programmer's judgement should never have been accepted. But it was.

THE FINGER OF BLAME

All too often, rotten old programs are preserved because everyone else is afraid of what will happen if the programmers attempt to modify them. Because the programmers have done a third-rate job, the keying operators are forced to live with an obsolete design. They try their best to perform error-prone activities-- tasks that would have been done better by the computer. When an installation reaches this stage, management has lost control. In their stead, the programmers-- and the worst ones, at that--are effectively running the installation.

As if this loss of control were not sufficiently bad, such programmers typically accuse the people in data preparation of being "stupid" and "poorly motiv- ated." Name-calling never adds to the morale of an installation, though in truth, these descriptions apply to the name-callers themselves. As an old peasant proverb puts it,

WHEN SOMEONE POINTS AN ACCUSING FINGER,
LOOK WHERE THE SECOND FINGER POINTS.

USING OR CREATING SUBLISTS

Another situation that violates our rule of thumb involves lists with substructure. Consider the follow- ing entries for a telephone directory:

MR. ALPHONSE ROGER GLADSTONE 402 845 6744

MS. RONA DELICIA GARFINKELSTEIN 212 536 3029

Because both area codes and exchange codes are to be used as key items, these messages can be considered to contain *seven* items in sequence:

gender first middle last area exchange number

Even so, they really don't seem that long. Why not?

The secret to the coherence of this list is the *substructure* based on commonly recognized groupings. An alternative syntactic description of this list is:

name phone-number

where name is decomposed into

gender first middle last

and phone-number, into

area exchange number

This hierarchic description corresponds more closely to the psychological reality of the sequencing. It contains far less possible variation than some other, randomly ordered list of the same seven items, such as

middle exchange first number gender last area

Trying to memorize this sequence will show the skeptic what is meant by "psychological reality," and why it is important in determining the *effective* length of a sequence.

USING OR CREATING ITEM IDENTIFICATION

It is still possible that the name and phone-number lists could be entered out of sequence. Checking their order is an essential feature of a reliable design. Fortunately, the different nature of the two lists provides useable redundancy for checking.

The names are primarily alphabetic and often longer than four characters. The parts of the phone-number, on the other hand, are largely numeric, and have invariant lengths (in the USA) of 3, 3, and 4. Such regularities can easily be built into a recognition program that will protect against permutations of the proper sequence.

Useable redundancy does not always exist in lists. If we are sufficiently concerned about the consequences of misinterpretation, however, we may be willing to *add* redundancy to make explicit identification possible, as in

ORDER: CUST=2345 QTY=3 PROD=3456

Alternatively, we might use a partial combination of the two techniques, as in

```
CUST=2345   3   PROD=3456
```

Once we have such redundancy, we can protect
against erroneous sequences--or, we may no longer
need sequence at all. But that leads us to the next
chapter topic, *identified messages.*

A SUMMARY OF EXPECTED ATTRIBUTES

The following is a simplified multidimensional view of
the normal attributes which the designer can expect
when specifying the positional technique. The designer must calculate or otherwise estimate the more accurate attributes for his particular implementation in
order to compare this option against other design
alternatives.

PRODUCTIVITY

The user can avoid placement of data elements
into particular "geographic" positions (such as pre-
designated card columns or fields). This flexibility
saves "form filling" effort whose only justification
is often to make sure data elements are placed correctly. Positional determination of message content
can also save the need for explicit identifiers, thus
improving work flow for high volume message types.
Properly designed, positional messages can increase
operator comfort and productivity.

RELIABILITY

Although positional messages have inherent dangers
of misinterpretation, appropriate design can overcome
these dangers. In some cases, however, there will be
a direct trade-off between reliability and raw productivity. In such cases, the designer has to choose
the design that best achieves productivity in terms
of overall functional requirements.

PORTABILITY

Positional techniques are portable to most data

registration devices, but they can require added program logic for interpretation, as compared to fixed-
field data. Any additional program logic might have
to be maintained and converted when moving to a new
system, and such costs must be considered.

IMPLEMENTATION EASE

Analysis, design, and programming efforts may be
slightly increased, when compared with conventional
fixed-field designs. Training and testing effort will
depend on the exact design, but better human design
always reduces training.

HARDWARE RESOURCES

A few additional lines of code may be required,
but hardly enough to burden even the smallest of the
small computers or intelligent terminals. Transmission requirements may be reduced over fixed-field
systems.

SECURITY

Because the input devices or forms themselves do
not document the input formats, the untrained operator
or intruder is more likely to spring some trap--so
that unauthorized use of the system is detected.

EXTENDABILITY

In the positional environment, additional
message meanings can often be added to the format
without causing conflict with the existing structure.
If we have a list of two items, a third, optional item
can be added at the end and need not be considered at
all by those operators, or on those transactions, that
don't use it.

One limitation to such extension is the confusion
that may be caused by adding a high-frequency item
following a low-frequency one. If a new message

element represents some important activity, it may be present even when earlier items in the list are omitted. By adding such a high-frequency item to the end of the list, we force the use of missing-item symbols--thus getting increased errors and lower productivity.

One way out of this trap is to design the new message to be a *composition* of two subsequences--the old, well-learned sequence and a sequence of new items. In this way, learning about the new codes will not interfere with the previously learned material about the old.

DESIGN EXERCISES

1.   Rework Exercise 1 of Chapter 2 (page 52) using positional techniques. When you have completed this redesign, compare the two approaches and state the relative advantages of each. Then try to redesign the system to capture some of the best points of default and positional input systems.

2.   We want to design a system for entering lists of 12 numeric items. We wish to study various designs, including line lengths of 12, 6, 4, 3, and 2 items-- both with and without resynchronization.

Using your favorite programming language or charting technique, write a simple program to estimate the keying effort under each design. What approxima- tions and assumptions have gone into your model? In the light of these approximations and assumptions, how much credence should you place in the predicted results? How would you design a simple experiment to validate your models?

3.   We wish to compute estimates of keystrokes and transmission loading per transaction of the following message design. An order entry system uses up to five items per message, according to the following formal syntax:

customer-number {{discount} quantity} catalog {color}

Compute your estimates based on the following information:

1. customer-number   *always present, 1-4 characters, with each length
equally likely*

2. discount   *present in 3% of the orders
with half 1-character and
half 2-character*

3. quantity   *defaults to 1 in 75% of
orders, 1-digit in another
20%, 2-digit in 4%, 3-digit
in 1%*

4. catalog   *always present, always six
digits*

5. color   *present in 5% of orders,
1-4 digits with each length
equally likely*

Because the catalog number is always present and always six digits (while no other item has more than four digits), it can be used as an internal synchronization point. Some typical input messages are as follows:

2345 15 567890 12

2345 12 15 567890 12

2345 12 15 567890

2345 15 567890

2345 567890

After completing your computation, compare your estimates with a conventional fixed-field design. Also, list the assumptions that underlie your computation.

4. Design an adequate set of test data for the input design of Exercise 3. Justify each case, and each error case, as well as the cases you excluded from the test. Based on what you learn in designing these tests, specify changes you would like to see made in the design.

Chapter IV

Identified Messages

Come, listen, my men, while I tell you again
    The five unmistakable marks
By which you may know, wheresoever you go,
    The warranted genuine Snarks.

Let us take them in order. The first is the taste,
    Which is meagre and hollow, but crisp:
Like a coat that is rather too tight in the waist,
    With a flavour of Will-o'-the-wisp.

Its habit of getting up late, you'll agree
    That it carries too far, when I say
That it frequently breakfasts at five-o'clock tea,
    And dines on the following day.

The third is its slowness in taking a jest.
    Should you happen to venture on one,
It will sigh like a thing that is deeply distressed:
    And will always look grave at a pun.

The fourth is its fondness for bathing-machines,
    Which it constantly carries about,
And believes that they add to the beauty of scenes--
    A sentiment open to doubt.

The fifth is ambition. It next will be right
    To describe each particular batch:
Distinguishing those that have feathers, and bite,
    From those that have whiskers, and scratch.

--*The Hunting of the Snark, Fit the Second*

Like Snarks, many data items can be recognized by a variety of "unmistakable marks" when they are seen in context. These marks may be either intrinsic, like the taste of a Snark or the form of a data item such as 27OCT33, or extrinsic, carried about external to the data item, like bathing machines or the "N=" in the item, "N=177". The former are called *self-ident-ified*; the latter, *explicitly-identified*. In either form, they are a powerful technique for input design-- a sentiment not open to doubt.

SELF-IDENTIFICATION

The interpretation of *self-identified* data items does not depend on position--either fixed or relative to other items. Indeed, the principal advantage of the method is the ability to place the same item in different positions on different occasions, or to use the position and identification as a check or synchronization point.

UNIQUENESS

The form of self-identifying data is designed to be unique, either within an entire message or between two known points. This unique form can then be used by a program to make correct interpretation without recourse to other information in the message--though internally stored information might be used. Consider these examples:

    123 4567 USA 0 23

    123 USA 4567 0 23

    123 4567 0 23 USA

Obviously, there are two characteristics which enable us to determine that USA has a particular meaning in all three different message formats, regardless of its position:

> It is alphabetic, while all other data are numeric.

> It is to be found in a programmed table of valid country codes, such as GB, USA, NL, F, J, AND, and CAN.

In designing self-identified data, we must be sure that the identification can *always* be made on the basis of characteristics alone. For instance, in the above example, there might be other alphabetic data permitted in the non-country fields, and some of it by chance may correspond to the country table, as in

    N 123 4567 USA 0 23

where the N is in fact a NO reply and is not the code for Norway. Another obvious case is AND, for Andorra, which might easily be taken for something else. In such cases, we must consider *explicit identifiers*-- which we will take up in a later section.

CONVENTIONAL SYMBOLS

Of course, the line between explicit and self-identifying components is not necessarily a clear one, which is why we consider them as two aspects of the same approach. This is especially true when we use *conventional* symbols attached to the data item, as in the following examples:

EXAMPLE	EXPLANATION AND COMMENT
25%	*Unmistakably and instantly recognizable as a percentage.*

EXAMPLE	EXPLANATION AND COMMENT
$25	*This or other national currency characters render the item unambiguously as money.*
34.50	*The decimal point (or comma in European notation) will often have a single meaning in the application, such as money amount.*
34.503	*The extra decimal place with the decimal point may render the meaning clear in another way--this might be a measured quantity, like weight.*
34,503	*The comma (or period in European systems) may distinguish a large amount from a long serial number of some kind. This symbol cannot be used safely if there is any chance of a number less than 1,000. Also, it cannot be used at all if the comma is used as a list delimiter, unless a space is* required *after each comma used as a list delimiter.*
34.7#	*This symbol is conventionally used in North America to indicate* weight *in some standard unit, like pounds or kilograms, when it follows the number.*
#347	*Preceding a number, and following a space, the "#" conventionally means an* identification number, *rather than an amount.*
@29.25	*"@" conventionally indicates a* price *in North America. The decimal point might be a useful redundancy, or might be omitted if the units are well understood.*
@USA	*Another meaning of "@" comes from the same English word, "at"--in this case meaning a* place.
37¢	*The cent symbol is often used to indicate* currency *in small denominations.*

EXAMPLE	EXPLANATION AND COMMENT
34?	*The question mark indicates* doubt *about something. Here, it could be a query such as, "Do we have 34 pieces in stock?" Alternatively, it could be used to indicate some uncertainty in the data item itself, in which case, the program might be called upon to double check, or to carry this uncertainty through further use of the datum.*
456-78-9876 456-9876	*The dash within a field conventionally indicates that the datum is some sort of* identification, *and not a quantity. A conventional length, or pattern, may give further clues to identity. For instance, American readers can tell at a glance which of these two examples is a telephone number and which is a Social Security number.*
096564	*The presence of an explicit leading zero often signals an* identifier, *rather than a quantity--except when used in computer-oriented, rather than people-oriented, forms.*
(402)788-2936	*Parentheses conventionally indicate some sort of* optional *information, or information which is* not as important *as other information to which it is attached. This example, to Americans, clearly indicates an "area code"-- which need not be dialed on local calls--and thus the entire item is identified as a telephone number.*
34.50(A)	*This parenthesized symbol might be used to mean that this price of 34.50 applies only to class A customers.*
MR. JONES MS. JONES MISS JONES	*The title can indicate* gender; marital status *of women, in some cases (though what business is that of the comput-er?); and that a person's name is the*

EXAMPLE	EXPLANATION AND COMMENT
	following information (that is, it is used as a synchronization point).
29.8C 43cm 43cc 29.8kg	*Certain letters or letter combinations trailing a quantity have conventional meaning as units--in these examples, degrees Celsius, centimeters, cubic centimeters, and kilograms.*
43x27x12 2x4	*The "x" or special "times" sign is readily recognized to indicate* dimensions.
MILL ST. CORNER AVE.	Addresses *can often be recognized by one of a small number of (possibly abbreviated) symbols for street, avenue, boulevard, lane, row, highway, court, circle, and so forth. This symbol can then be taken as a synchronization point for the preceding information.*

CONVERSION OF EXISTING SYSTEMS

Many further examples could be given. The designer would do well to examine existing practice in the industry in question to discover conventions that will be widely understood. By formal grammatical analysis, it should be possible to design an unambiguous system that is as natural as the following:

```
MR. CHARLES EVANS HUGHES
97 PARK LANE
PRAIRIE HOME, NE 68505   (403)821-3176
15%           @WHSE

100#    683-921-2    @37.26    RED
30      2x4x16       491-864-0      @3.95
```

Any American reader, at least, should be able to understand the entire message without further explanation--and so should a reasonably effective computer program.

This principle has proved useful in designing conversion of non-computerized records to machine-readable formats. With proper analysis, we can usually permit keying from the records as they stand, without form-filling or encoding.

In an off-line operation, the entire file is passed through a program representing the most likely interpretation. As indicated in Figure 4.1, this "sieve" should substantially reduce the number of cases to be investigated by succeeding stages. In an on-line operation, one message at a time can be interpreted as keyed, with immediate feedback for operator confirmation or interpretation.

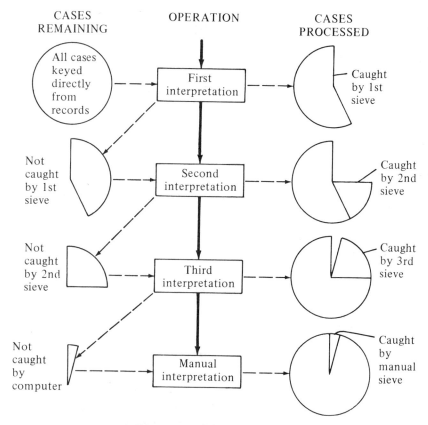

Figure 4.1 Conversion of an existing file by successive attempts at automatic interpretation of identified items.

The principal advantage of on-line operation is
the operator confirmation. The principal advantage of
the off-line operation is not having to program all
sieves in advance. After the first interpretation has
been programmed and run, the second interpretation can
be derived by investigating those records not yet
caught. This stepwise procedure may eliminate unneed-
ed programming. On the other hand, if the files are
large, the cost of programming such simple "sieves"
should be small in relation to the cost of complete
encoding.

SELF-IDENTIFYING DATES

Probably no other data element has such wide use and
such wide variation in format as *dates*. One of our
manufacturing clients found in a survey of computer
programs that there were 37 separate date printing
routines in their library, which produced at least 18
different date formats!

DATE FORMATS

Some of the many date formats are listed below,
to indicate the opportunities for either creative
input design or disaster--depending on our approach:

EXAMPLE	EXPLANATION AND COMMENT
1978	*The "19" as the leading two digits, and the four-digit length, spots this as a year. (No doubt the computer industry is going to collapse on 1 January 2000--ask your programmers why. Forecasting programs have already begun to collapse--1975 was a bad year for 25-year forecasts.)*
31/6/79	*The two slashes, the three sets of digits (1 to 31, 1 to 12, 70 to 80?) can be used not only to examine validity, but also to interpret the meaning of the datum.*

6/31/79   *There is ambiguity in the order of*
4/12/81   *month-day-year, and many variations*
12/4/81   *exist, not all of which can be dis-*
           criminated on the basis of the format
           or the range.

12 APRIL 1981   *Names of months, and/or recog-*
                nizable years, can be used as synch-
                ronization points.

12.4.81   *Decimal points are sometimes used*
           within dates as field separators.
           Since no decimal number can have this
           form, and since sterling currency is
           at long last disappearing from the
           Empire, this is relatively unambig-
           uous as a date--though part numbers
           sometimes have such a form.

12.IV.81   *The European railway date system has*
4.XII.81   *a lot to recommend it, such as dis-*
           ambiguation of the month field and
           day field, plus a simple recognition
           by way of the limited permitted set
           of Roman numerals.

4XII81   *The periods (or slashes) may be elim-*
2IX83   *inated when the Roman month is used,*
21X83   *though the I and 1 are relatively*
           easy to confuse in reading.

6/1979   *Sometimes only month and year are*
6/79   *given, as in an estimated shipping*
           date or completion date. In this
           case, the period is not usually
           suitable.

1977/1979 *Approximate dates have many forms,*
1977/79   *such as beginning and ending year,*
1977-1979 *but may be ambiguous as to inclusion*
           or exclusion of one or both end
           points.

21-30 AUG *The dash is more conventionally used*
           with days of the month to indicate an
           interval.

TUES 4/12 *Names of days of the week can often*

EXAMPLE	EXPLANATION AND COMMENT

be used as synchronization symbols or check words for dates which might not otherwise be recognized, particularly in industries where day-of-week is important.

RECOGNITION PROGRAMS

Many more examples could be given. While for output purposes it may be well for an installation to standardize on one or perhaps two date forms, there is usually no reason to restrict inputs so narrowly. It is relatively easy to program a date recognition routine that can be used in a variety of applications, and which will give the operators lots of room to adopt a comfortable style.

Where potentially ambiguous forms are used, feedback can clarify whether, for example, we meant to say 6/12/81 or 12/6/81--even when permitting such unambiguous forms as 6/13/81 and 13/6/81. We can design such a recognition routine for operator comfort or for very conservative sheltering against errors. On the other hand, operator comfort is often our best insurance against high error rates.

RELATIVE DATES

One way to increase operator comfort is to employ *relative* dates. For example, in a manufacturing operation, the completion date of an item now on the floor might be most easily apprehended by the workers as 1, 2, or 3 days *from now*. Or, the completion date might be expressed relative to a *scheduled* completion date, with -2 meaning two days early and +2 meaning two days late.

INTERNATIONAL STANDARD DATES

Operator "comfort" depends on the training and experience of the operator. A good example of the effect of training is the international standard for dates and times for computer use--a standard set without much concern for the humans who use computers.

The standard is based on descending order of time units--year-month-day-hour-minute-second. For example:

1978-12-31

781231

780614.140229

These forms are unambiguous, compact, and simple to compare for time relationships--for the computer. The inexperienced operator may find that such forms are very difficult to use without error. Yet most people working around computers for a while become so accustomed to these forms that they begin to consider them "natural."

EXPLICIT IDENTIFIERS

As we start to use special key symbols which may not be entirely conventional, we move into the area of *explicit identifiers.*

REMOVING AMBIGUITY

Recall, for example, the ambiguous case

N   123   4567   USA

in which N could mean either NO or NORWAY. We can disambiguate by adding an explicit identifier to the nation item, as in

N   NATION=USA   123   4567

Other forms of key symbol for "nation" could be used:

N   N=USA 123   4567

Notice that the "N=" key symbol cannot be confused with the N for NORWAY or the N for NO, because of the overall format of the item.

Another way to disambiguate the message is by attaching the explicit identifier to the reply, instead of the nation, as in:

        REPLY=N USA 123 4567

Again, many alternative key symbols are available,
such as in

        ?N USA 123 4567

CHOOSING IDENTIFIERS

    When using self-identifying items, we could foll-
ow conventional usage in designing the input, but how
do we decide which explicit identifiers to use, when
the choice is so great? The choice involves trade-off
or balancing of many factors, including

> *programming ease*
>
> *volume of input*
>
> *experience of operators*
>
> *need for redundancy to aid error detection
> and correction*
>
> *need for readability*
>
> *need for flexibility, as in input order,
> or in correction*

RANDOM ORDER OF ITEMS

    Let us consider a few cases in some depth, before
examining more general choice procedures. A familiar
example of explicitly identified data (to PL/I users)
is the GET DATA (and PUT DATA) format. To take a
simple case, the statement:

    GET DATA(DEPRECIATION, INTEREST, RISK);

permits the input of DEPRECIATION, INTEREST, and RISK
in any order, as in

    DEPRECIATION=.08 INTEREST=.075 RISK=.22;

    RISK=.22 INTEREST=.075 DEPRECIATION=.08;

    INTEREST=.08 DEPRECIATION=.12 RISK=.31;

This ability to give input with meaningful names and
in any order is a great help to the inexperienced or

casual user. Inasmuch as the GET DATA routines are
built into the PL/I language, the programming is much
simpler than we might expect for such a powerful
device.

CORRECTION BY REPETITION

GET DATA, like other explicit identifier schemes,
permits *repetitions* of the same explicitly identified
item--which is useful for corrections. If the user
has typed

DEPRECIATION=.08 INTEREST=.075 RISK=.22

and just then realizes that DEPRECIATION should have
been .12, the correction can be made simply by typing

DEPRECIATION=.12;

after what has already been typed on the line. Only
the semicolon terminates the message, so any number
of corrections can be made up until the time the semicolon is typed. When the input message is long, when
the operators are not very experienced or are prone to
errors for other reasons, and especially when back-
space-type-over resynchronization is not available,
this correction feature can save a great deal of rekeying and aggravation.

CARRYOVERS

Another feature that GET DATA shares with many
explicit identification schemes is the possibility of
omitting items. The system designer can harness this
feature in a number of ways. For instance, it may be
used to permit *carryover* of values from the previous
input case or cases. This is a very common situation
in simulations, which have numerous parameters that
would be tedious to re-enter for each case, yet where
each case is different from the previous in but a few
parameters. Using GET DATA, only the *changed* parameters need be entered. In effect, this is a method
of *defaults*--using the *previous* case for the default.
In a batch operation, there is a danger that the cases
might be used out of sequence, thus destroying the

default structure--rather a limitation on the technique than a prohibition.

  In commercial applications, many similar carry-
overs exist. For instance, in keying line items from
an invoice, all of the indicative information from the
invoice heading is usually carried over, and within
the invoice there may be carryover in such items as
descriptions, discount codes, and even quantities.
Consider the following order-entry situation:

```
DATE: 4 JULY 1976        ORDER NUMBER Q10315

THE LIBERTY FIREWORK WAREHOUSE

1776 INDEPENDENCE AVENUE

DECLARATION, WASHINGTON 99595     DISCOUNT 18%

QTY   CATALOG        DESCRIPTION      SIZE    COLOR

12    SKY-39761  SKYROCKETS-DELUXE LARGE    RED
12    SKY-39785  SKYROCKETS-DELUXE LARGE    WHITE
12    SKY-39793  SKYROCKETS-DELUXE LARGE    BLUE
12    SKY-39754  SKYROCKETS-DELUXE SMALL    BLUE
```

  This order displays a great deal of redundant
carryover. In fact, we seldom see an order written
like this, but more often see orders with a liberal
use of ditto marks, as in the following:

```
QTY   CATALOG        DESCRIPTION      SIZE    COLOR

12    SKY-39761  SKYROCKETS-DELUXE LARGE    RED
 "     "   39785  "                  "      WHITE
 "     "   39793  "                  "      BLUE
 "     "   39754  "               SMALL     "
```

  Orders and other repetitive documents are often
written like this unless the computer people--with
great cost, strain, and bad feelings--have forced
everyone to conform to "what the computer must have."
Instead of forcing people into unnatural acts, why not
draw upon this "folk wisdom" in designing the input?

  In a well-designed system based on self-identifying and explicitly identified items, with carryover, the entire order can be punched like this:

    4 JULY 1976   ORDNO=Q10513   ORDNO=Q10315

    THE LIBERTY FIREWORK WAREHOUSE

    1776 INDEPENDENCE AVE. DECLARATION, WA 18%

    12 SKY-39761 SKYROCKETS-DELUXE LARGE RED

    -39785 WHITE -39793 BLUE -39754 SMALL

Notice how the operator detected a keying error in the order number and corrected it simply by tacking the correct value on the end of the line.

SELECTING THE METHOD OF IDENTIFICATION

After deciding that some form of identified code is needed, the designer must narrow down to a specific choice of *method* of identification. The first choice is between self-identifying and explicitly identified codes. Once this decision is made, there is still the choice of specific symbols to use.

SELF-IDENTIFICATION ADVANTAGES

Briefly, the advantages of self-identification over explicit identification are these:

less effort in keying stages

less form-filling and data collection effort

generally less data to transmit

less training, in many cases

less documentation, in many cases

EXPLICIT IDENTIFICATION ADVANTAGES

On the other hand, the advantages of explicit identification over self-identification are these:

a. Programming may be simpler.

b. The sequence of data elements may be more flexible. This flexibility may be especially advantageous when using forms from varied sources or forms not intended for computer input at all. Some of the less explicit forms may be restricted to certain areas of the message--for example, to certain message lines or after certain synchronization symbols.

c. Design is easier, especially for adding element types or new values to existing elements. With self-identification, the ability to identify uniquely may be highly context dependent (hence the restriction to certain message areas). Self-identification could be lost in unanticipated ways when changes are made in "other" parts of the message.

d. Messages will be more readable and interpretable by human beings, especially those not concerned with the messages every working day. Certain well-known self-identification conventions, however, may prove more readable than more explicit but less familiar forms of identification.

e. It may be easier to learn to write codes in an explicit format than to learn rules about restrictions on data content and sequence. Both this and the previous advantage may be lost if "shorthand" identification symbols are overused in an effort to reduce keying or transmission.

f. More possibility exists for permitting alternate forms of the same identification symbols. Alternate forms tend to reinforce advantages (d) and (e) at the expense of (a)--simplified programming. For instance, a common convention permits either the full identification symbol or its first character, as in

    INTEREST=.08   DISCOUNT=.075

    I=.08   D=.075

As the number of identifications grows, however, this abbreviation technique quickly runs into conflicts.

g. Added redundancy gives added protection against misinterpretation caused by corruption of the message part--either from keying error or misreading of handwriting. Programmed logic to detect or automatically correct such errors will be easier to write if the key symbols are designed with protection in mind.

MAKING THE CHOICE

As a rough rule of thumb, *explicit* data tend to be used

for low volume data items

for exceptional data items within a message

for data requiring an exceptionally high probability of correct input

On the other hand, *implicit* forms tend to be used

for high volume items

when the people using them will get plenty of practice (perhaps 100 times per working day)

when the forms are so natural that they don't require much practice.

In general, the designer should think first about implicit identification, which is always desirable if it actually applies. If no implicit identification exists, or if ambiguities are likely to arise from overuse of implication, the designer should then consider making some or all items explicitly identified.

It's important not to dismiss self-identification too casually. In our experience, there are a surprising number of codes that turn out to be self-identifying, even though they may be written on the source documents in irregular sequences. In a large conversion of pre-computer archives or catalogs, a little programming can save a lot of coding, transcription, punching, repunching, and general headaches. Therefore, a little headstrain by the designer in advance will save lots of aspirin in the end.

QUANTIFICATION EXAMPLE: THE ONE DOZEN ORDER

In Chapter 2, Figure 2.1 (page 31), we estimated the performance of four alternative methods of entering an order quantity for a wholesale drug company. The method of calculation was based on a *frequency distribution* of the various order quantities. To simplify the calculation, not every order quantity was tabulated in the frequency distribution. Instead, only four *categories* were used--the quantity 12, all one-digit quantities, all 2-digit quantities other than 12, and all 3-digit quantities.

THE STANDARD ORDERING UNIT

Such lumping of the various cases often simplifies the calculation, but sometimes conceals other structure in the true frequency distribution--structure that can be used to good advantage in the design. It's always a good idea for the designer to look at some of the data, and not just at summaries that are supposed to characterize it.

In the drug company situation, for instance, the 2-digit codes were most frequent, after the 12's. Closer inspection of the actual data revealed that the reason for this high frequency was the prevalance of even dozen orders--24, 36, 48, and so forth. Using this observation and the idea of identified codes, the designer was able to produce an alternative system which proved quite competitive with the simple variable-field default design (case d) of Figure 2.1.

Because of standard packing practice in the industry, almost all orders are in even dozens. Therefore, the *dozen* can be used as the *standard ordering unit*. As the standard ordering unit, it needs no explicit identification. When there is an odd lot (non-dozen) order, on the other hand, an identifying character is prefixed to the order quantity to indicate that it is *units, not dozens*. Although no symbol is completely satisfactory, the "#" seems to work reasonably well, for it can be read as "number"--from which it is a short mental step to "number of" or "quantity."

Under this system, messages would be interpreted as follows:

MESSAGE	INTERPRETATION
1 XYZ	*1 dozen of product XYZ (12 units)*
#1 ABC	*1 unit of product ABC*
#2 ABC	*2 units of product ABC*
2 RST	*2 dozen of product RST (24 units)*
#24 RST	*24 units of product RST (an alternative but longer form for the preceding entry)*

Once the operators become adapted to this method, within a fixed-field environment 1 through 9 dozen will require only 2 keystrokes--1 for quantity and 1 for skipping the field. One-digit *unit* orders will take 3 keystrokes (#, digit, skip), and 2-digit unit orders will take 4 keystrokes.

One interesting sidelight of this investigation was that the *only* 3-digit orders in the old system were *even dozen orders*. Each such order could thus be accomplished with 3 keystrokes--and the fixed-field width required only 3 positions.

KEYSTROKES

Using these figures, we can compute an average of about 2.1 keystrokes, as shown in Figure 4.2--not nearly as good as the best pure default system (.4 keystrokes for method (d) of Figure 2.1). Fortunately, we are never restricted to "pure" systems, and the second part of Figure 4.2 shows the expected keystrokes from a *combined* system.

In this second system design, the most frequent case--one dozen--is the default. This simple addition to the design reduces the average keystrokes dramatically to about .4--essentially the same as method (d) of Figure 2.1. We must be wary of making conclusions not warranted by the accuracy of our estimation models, and certainly any difference between this design and (d) is too small to mean anything about the difference

Input case	Frequency (f)	Dozens with # on exceptions		With addition of 1 dozen default	
		n	f × n	n	f × n
12	.85	2	1.70	0	0.00
24, 36, . . .	.08	2	.16	2	.16
1 digit	.05	3	.15	3	.15
other 2-digit	.01	4	.04	4	.04
3-digit even doz.	.01	3	.03	3	.03
Average keystrokes			2.08		.38

Figure 4.2   Estimated keystrokes for self-identifying dozens system, and with default of one dozen added.

in their keying productivities.

ERRORS

On the other hand, an analysis of their *error* properties may show significant differences, even when productivity in the raw form is the same. Since errors result in lost productivity, that is where we should concentrate our attention even if we think productivity is our "only" goal.

Based on keystrokes, the error rates of the two methods would be roughly the same. But the new system design happens to eliminate some *difficult mental calculations* on the part of the operators--multiplying by 12 when orders are specified in dozens (as they customarily are). Arithmetic like this is not what we mean when we speak of allowing the operators to think. Clearly, this is a step the computer can do much more reliably than any human, so allocating this step to the computer brings the error rate well below that predicted by the number of keystrokes.

GETTING BEHIND THE DATA

In this situation, a little time spent on the floor of the warehouse uncovered a number of facts about life in the underworld--facts not previously known to the systems analyst:

All items were stored in boxes of 12.

When an odd order was received, a box was broken to get the necessary items.

Many items were almost never *ordered in odd lots.*

Virtually all bins contained broken boxes.

Broken boxes were frequently picked by mistake as full boxes--which made the customers angry.

Pickers often failed to see a broken box in a bin and so unnecessarily broke another.

A substantial stock was in broken boxes.

Shelf life of the products was not long, and was even shorter when a box was opened.

It is insufficient to know the *frequency* of error. To design properly, we must also know the *consequences* of error. The design of the previous input system at this firm was largely responsible for the broken box situation. In that system, the most frequent error was failing to multiply by 12. Each time this error was made, a box was broken and the customer received a short shipment.

In the "dozens" system, the most frequent error may be dropping the "#". In that case, 12 will be shipped instead of 1--which will not cause any boxes to be broken. With the one dozen default, a plain 1 could be prohibited altogether--which would elimin- ate the majority of errors caused by dropping the "#".

In the remaining error conditions, the pharmacist may simply accept an overshipment. At worst, the pharmacist can return the surplus to the driver. In either case, the sick people who are waiting for medications will not suffer from a short shipment. Truly ridiculous overorders--like 10 dozen of a slow-moving item--can be screened out by various limit checks. A variety of other improvements are possible, based on the warehouse observations, but the lesson of the simplified example is clear:

An information system is just that--information. The real system is out there, beyond the scope of the data processing department. No savings in data processing can match the potential benefits of good data design for the real system. Therefore, the good designer will never forget:

GET BEHIND THE DATA TO THE FACTS.

A SUMMARY OF EXPECTED ATTRIBUTES

The following is a simplified multidimensional view of the normal attributes which the designer can expect when specifying the technique of self-identifying or explicitly identified data. The designer must calculate the more accurate attributes for his particular implementation in order to compare this option against other design alternatives.

PRODUCTIVITY

Identified messages tend to improve *total* productivity when used in appropriate message situations. The *apparent* extra effort due to the redundancy involved tends to repay itself quickly, because of the following factors:

ease of learning the rules, and remembering them

prevention of errors--which would cause delays and extra work--arising from the use of "natural" codes with more explicit meanings

faster keying of familiar combinations

ability to provide inputs in "natural" order, which may change from message to message ability to pick up data directly from "natural" sources, without "recoding" or rewriting onto a "computer form"

redundancy which allows stronger error detection/ correction logic to be applied, which in turn increases human productivity

possiblity of large savings through the use of defaults and avoidance of fixed fields

RELIABILITY

Identified codes generally have a high reliability, because they prevent errors in the first instance, and can be used in many situations to detect and correct errors that do occur. They are generally natural to read, which brings the human being into the prevention/detection/correction process.

PORTABILITY

If the identified codes use numerous special characters not found on standard input devices, portability can be adversely affected. Characters such as "?", "%", and "¢" are not available on low-cost devices--though the situation is improving rapidly.

Sometimes a good substitute can be found, particularly if an "overstrike" capability exists--either through overprinting or overwriting on a video unit. For instance, a passable "¢" can be created by overstriking "c" and "/", giving "¢"--though possibly at the expense of additional programming.

Overstruck characters can have the opposite effect on portability, for several reasons:

They are forbidden on certain hardware.

They can conflict with the use of backspace for other purposes, such as correction.

Operating system software may not be able to handle them, even when they are permitted by hardware.

IMPLEMENTATION EASE

Fully customized self-identifying systems can engender large programming costs. These costs need not be incurred all at once, however, if the system is developed in stages. Explicitly identified codes tend to be less costly, particularly if some consistent form (such as "name=value") is used throughout. When the programming language provides such a feature as PL/I's GET DATA (to read "A=2" type input), implementation costs can actually be cheaper than other systems.

HARDWARE RESOURCES

Identified data may require hardware capable of handling a variety of special characters (or overstruck characters). Transmission requirements may be either increased or decreased, depending on the actual design. In order to interpret identified data, additional storage may be necessary, but not enough to be critical.

SECURITY

The naturalness of the codes makes it more likely that a casual onlooker could understand them. On the other hand, this naturalness implies that trained people will not need a handbook for input of codes. Persons authorized to use the system know what they need to know by training and experience. Unauthorized users will have no easily accessible written descriptions of how to (mis) use the system.

EXTENDABILITY

Identified data tend to allow markedly greater freedom to extend, for it is rather easy to ensure that ambiguities will not be introduced when new codes are added. The ability to use any order of entry means that new codes can be added at any convenient point in the message, or at several points for different circumstances.

DESIGN EXERCISES

1.   Rework Exercise 1 of Chapter 3 (page 83) using identified techniques. When you have completed this redesign, compare the two approaches and state the relative merits of each. Then try to redesign the system to capture some of the best points of all the techniques used thus far.

2.   Describe the parameters you would need to make a first-order estimate of the keying productivity and error rates for the "firework" order-entry application described in this chapter. Describe some variants of the design you would like to consider to improve these performance figures. State the assumptions that would enter into your estimates, and show how a calculation might be performed.

3.   Given the input message with the following 6 items:

QUANTITY	DISCOUNT	SIZE	PRICE	CATALOG	COLOR
24	12%	3x5	$1.25	X-39-18	RED

show how you would estimate the productivity rates under the conditions that:

  a.   Fields could be corrected by simply rekeying them later in the message.

  b.   Each item has its distinct probability of error.

  c.   Each item has its distinct probability of being omitted to take a default (except for the catalog-number).

4.   Show how the above simulation could be compared with a system using the same 6 items, but in which a pure *positional* approach is taken. Corrections are made by cancelling an *entire line* whenever a keying error is detected--to resynchronize to the beginning. Be sure your simulation takes into account that different orderings of the 6 items will produce different productivity rates, in view of corrections made necessary by point (b) above. Discuss this phenomenon in relation to design.

5. Using a telephone directory, design an input format and suggest suitable logic to interpret each part of the information. Consider the following data elements:

> name: first, middle (or initial), and last
>
> title, if any
>
> street address
>
> building name
>
> route number
>
> floor or apartment number
>
> postal box
>
> non-person entries (Ltd., Inc., & Co., Assoc.,..)

The objective should be to design a series of "sieve" programs to extract as much data automatically as is consistent with economy, using optical character recognition equipment for original input. Also, non-recognizable elements should be clearly identified, and not recorded in error. Estimate the cost of the system, compared with completely coded conversion.

6. Redesign the above system to *minimize the amount of keying,* as well as the amount of time or work needed to evaluate what should be keyed (under the assumption that OCR equipment is not available or not suitable for this material).

Consider teaching the operator to abbreviate simple codes for frequent data types, either automatically or by a training procedure. Look for other structural redundancy, such as duplication of last names, that could lead to minimal keying with proper design. Note that the operator should never have to look up codes on an instruction sheet in a well-designed system. Use what is on the input document, or whatever will be easy to remember without tables.

7. Design, for the above example, ways of ensuring
the accuracy of keyed data, without using proof-
reading or repetitive keying. The objective is not
perfection, but just a reasonable probability of
avoiding errors, detecting important ones, and correcting errors by program wherever possible.

      Hint: *First* minimize the probability of error,
then minimize the amount of work while retaining the
low error probabilities.

Chapter V

Repetition

Just the place for a Snark! I have said it twice:
That alone should encourage the crew.
Just the place for a Snark! I have said it thrice:
What I tell you three times is true.

--The Hunting of the Snark, Fit the First

What we tell three times may not be true, but it may
be a more *reliable* rendering of something we are trying to say.

REPETITION OR REPETITION?

In natural systems, repetition is universal. For
a bird, finding a mate is too important to be left to
a single performance of a song. To a flower, propaga-
tion of the species is too important to be left to a
single seed. To our bodies, the transmission of ner-
vous messages is too important to be left to a single
cell.

WHY REPEAT?

In artificial systems, too, repetition is used to achieve reliable performance. Consider the time-honored principle of the telegraph system, requiring the repetition of abstract codes at the end of each telegram. The reasoning behind this tested practice is worth restating:

The error frequency for such data is high. Some errors are to be expected in almost every telegram, arising from human and equipment failure.

Whereas simple errors in plain language text can often be corrected at sight (JANBARY becomes JANUARY, PAMYENT becomes PAYMENT), coded information lacks the necessary redundancy for such correction (35469 becomes 34569??).

The 100% redundancy is simple to create. It requires only repetition of a previous task, which is far easier than check digit calculation, for example.

Detection of errors requires a simple comparative observation by human beings.

Once an error is detected, correction can frequently be made on the basis of reasonability checks. Compare, for instance, the dates FEB 31 and FEB 21. We can easily see which is likely to be right (if any), and why.

In other cases, the recipient can correct a detected error by refering to supplementary data. In the worst cases, retransmission is possible and may be requested soon after the message.

BRINGING REPETITION TO THE COMPUTER

In data processing, control of error-prone messages by means of repetitive keying from one source document is still common today--usually employing two work processes, two operators, and two machines. The most obvious disadvantage of this process is that only a single set of data is made available to the *computer*

for evaluation. Any correction routines must thus be
entirely human, even when the computer might be able
to do a superior job. Why not keep the principal
advantages of repetition by making the repeated data
available to the computer to analyze?

Why not indeed? Because we're still stuck in the
mental swamp of punch card thinking. In the old days,
the "unit record" was all we had. At least as much
effort went into squeezing input requirements below
80 columns as went into building the Great Wall of
China.

And why were we limited to 80 columns? For some
reason, the size of the original card was chosen to
match the old US dollar bill--a clever way to induce
respect and prevent mutilation. The number of punches
was limited by the size holes and spacing needed by
the crude punching and reading mechanisms. Even worse,
many of the 80 columns were reserved for punching
intermediate results--because there was no memory.

Nowadays, we need no longer be restricted by 100-
year old technology, or by the size of a 19th century
dollar bill. We can readily put the results of repeated keying into computer input, thus minimizing, if
not eliminating, human intervention, special "verifying" machines, and double handling of source materials.
Examples can be as simple as these:

234 234 part-number   (quantity 234 is repeated)

customer-no 2.98 2.98 (amount 2.98 is repeated)

EXCEPTIONAL REPETITION

Repetition, as we see in the above examples, does
not have to be specified for all fields in an input
message. Nor does it even have to be included in all
messages of a certain type. Rather than choose blindly for complete repetition, the designer can substantially reduce the effective cost of repetition by
applying some forethought.

EVALUATING REPETITION

In one system, less than 2% of all messages containing a quantity data element were longer than one digit (10 to 9,999). The other 98% were single digit quantities (1 to 9). The system was designed so that all 2-digit or longer quantities required repetition, so that the largest and most critical quantities were well protected.

How much did this protection cost? The average repeated quantity was no more than 3 digits long, and the average total message was 45 characters. Thus, in 2% of the messages, the length was increased from 45 to 48 characters. In the other 98%, the length was unchanged. The average length was thus increased to 45.06 characters, or 0.1%.

The cost of this repetition was thus essentially zero, but what was its *value*? The designer can evaluate exceptional repetition by considering the following questions:

a.   *What is the likelihood of each error?*

b.   *What are the consequences of each error?*

c.   *In the light of (a) and (b), is there some place where disproportionate returns can be obtained from extra keying?*

DISPROPORTIONATE RETURNS

What is meant by "disproportionate returns"? In the example under consideration, errors in large quantity order lines were more critical than errors in small ones, for three reasons:

The degree of error could be larger when a tens, hundreds, or thousands digit is changed.

These errors affected the larger customers, who were considered more important.

They were more likely to produce temporary out-of-stock conditions, as when 300 was changed to

800, followed by overstock conditions when the extra 500, in this example, were returned about the same time the automatic reorder came in.

IS IT EXTRA WORK (FOR ME)?

Unfortunately, the separation of function in the typical large organization often prevents the designer from acting on this kind of information. In one client's office where exceptional repetition was proposed, the head of data preparation refused to go along--because her section was measured on "errors per 1000 transactions punched" and "transactions per operator per day."

Adding any kind of repetition would have increased the number of errors detected at the computer, while decreasing the number of transactions produced by each operator each day--making data preparation look bad. Yet the change would have vastly improved operations in sales and inventory. Lacking an overall view of the functions of the system, this client saw repetitive keying as just so much "extra work."

DEMAND REPETITION

It isn't always convenient or psychologically realistic to expect people to remember rules such as "key all 2- to 4-digit numbers twice," especially if the rule applies only to rather infrequent cases. Therefore, a good system will be able to *demand* repetition for those data elements which *should* have it.

A DEMAND-DRIVEN DIALOGUE

Consider the following on-line dialogue:

INTERACTION	*REMARKS*
3 CLAVICYTHERIUMS	*No repetition required in small amount.*

234 RHYTHMOMETERS	*Large number, but repetition has been forgotten.*
PLEASE CONFIRM THIS LARGE QUANTITY	*Computer prompts (and incidentally teaches)*
234	*Human repeats the exceptional quantity demanded by the prompt.*
OK	*Computer agrees that amounts check.*
432 432 OPHICLEIDES	*Operator has learned to avoid prompting message.*
6668 668 ORGANOPHONES	*Operator makes a simple error.*
IS 668 CORRECT? (Y/N)	*Computer guesses lower of the two quantities.*
6668	*Operator repeats correct quantity.*
6,668 ACCEPTED	*Computer confirms, because value is equal to previously keyed value.*

Demand repetition is yet another example in which we take advantage of the human ability to adapt. Early in the introduction of such a system, operators will slow down because of increased interaction. If the system has been properly defined, however, operators will quickly improve.

The larger the volume, the faster the operators learn. If there is only one kind of input, a few minutes on-line should be sufficient to achieve mastery. On the other hand, for many small volume jobs, the slight increase in interaction time will not matter, so in either case, the increased accuracy is essentially without cost.

VARIANTS

In demand repetition, the designer has a number of variations to consider:

the condition under which the prompt is given-- any suspected inconsistency or indication of potentially large consequences can be a trigger

the response necessary to obtain acceptance

the nature of messages from computer to operator--emphasis can be on learning or on getting the present case right

Because of the large number of variations, computing the effect of demand repetition is likely to require a simulation. Learning, however, may be difficult to simulate, if we must know the exact manner in which better performance will be achieved. On the other hand, learning permits each operator to settle down, eventually, to an unprompted state of productivity. Therefore, if we are interested only in final results, we need not simulate learning at all.

BATCH ENVIRONMENTS

Is demand repetition limited to on-line data entry? Not at all. In fact, in "normal" batch editing, *every* value that fails to pass edit tests is sent back with a demand for rekeying--though the original value is seldom sent back to the computer with the rekeyed value. Because such a demand forces a delay in processing, the edit program may sometimes decide to accept a suspicious value provisionally.

How does the designer decide which values to accept or reject? The choice of action depends on the trade-off between two costs:

the cost of error

the cost of delay

In an on-line data entry system, we can demand repetition with a delay measured in a few seconds or less. This delay is so small that essentially *any* error would be more costly. Therefore, in on-line systems, the designer has an easy job deciding when to reject a suspicious value.

In a batch system, the decision is more difficult,

but not impossible. Some designers assume that the
cost of error is always greater than the cost of
delay--their systems will reject anything suspicious.
Others make the reverse assumption--their systems will
accept errors that later prove costly.

The most common editing practice assumes error is
more critical than delay. In these systems, all actions are deferred and a listing is made of suspicious
inputs for off-line correction. Yet in many cases,
it will be cost-effective to attempt automatic correction to the most probable, or least dangerous, value.

MAKING REPETITION EFFECTIVE

Figure 5.1 shows a generalized model of repetition
used in input. The potential effectiveness of such a
system depends on the design of detector/corrector,
but also on the placement of the repeater and the
nature of the repetition process.

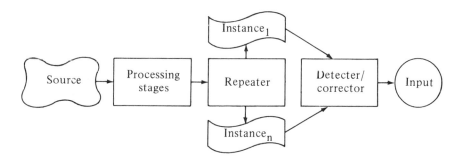

Figure 5.1 A model of the repetition process.

GET TO THE SOURCE

Repetition can never, by itself, help in controlling errors that occur *before* the repetition stage.
Consider the design of an input system for a furniture
factory. If the system is to know how many chairs
were manufactured, what kind of repetition helps ensure accurate counting?

If a certain batch contains 412 chairs, we would like that number, 412, to reach the computer. Suppose an inventory clerk counts 409 chairs and writes this count in two places on a "source" document. Will this duplicate writing protect against errors?

It *will* protect against errors that occur *after* the counting, such as:

the clerk miswriting one of the 409's

a data entry person misreading 409 as 407

an OCR device misreading 409 as 909

In no case, however, can the repetition help the computer obtain the correct number of chairs.

To eliminate *counting* errors, the duplication must be *earlier than the counting,* or *in the counting itself*, by some such means as

having two different clerks count the chairs

counting the chairs once and deriving another count from a tally of parts going into the chairs

having one clerk count twice, but by a different method each time

These forms of repetition would protect against the above errors, plus errors in the counting process itself. The moral for designers is clear:

ADD REDUNDANCY AS CLOSE TO THE SOURCE AS POSSIBLE

SOURCE OR SOURCE DOCUMENT?

There *are* instances in which the "source document" actually is the source, in some legal or conventional sense. A signed customer order represents a legal commitment, even if the customer wrote "3,000 kilograms" when he meant to write "3.000 kilograms." *Other* checking techniques could catch this customer's error, but simply keying "3,000 kilograms" two times will do no good whatsoever. And, while the customer is legally committed to paying for this order, he's not legally committed to being happy about it.

The very best designs obtain the needed repetition from the source--the *true* source. For instance, in phone orders, the operator's protocol, or script, may simply require that the customer be asked to repeat the quantity, or repeat if it seems extraordinary. With proper design, this repetition need not be offensive to the customer, and may even give the impression of thoroughness and care.

Such a telephone interaction meets three major points underlying the success of the repetition technique:

> *Have the human operator look at the source data a second time, or hear it a second time, before rekeying it.*

> *Obtain two machine-readable copies in case of operator error or any subsequent error such as keyboard fault, memory loss, or program failure.*

> *Place the repetition as close to the source as possible--in this case, at the source itself.*

INDEPENDENCE

Most existing systems fall short of the ideal of obtaining repetition from the true source. In these systems, the input designer has three lines of attack:

> *Try to approach the source more closely, even if the actual source cannot be reached.*

> *Use other techniques to combat errors, either preventing or detecting them.*

> *Make sure that whatever repetition is used is employed effectively.*

In general, the more *independence* among errors in the multiple input copies, the greater probability of detecting--and perhaps correcting--errors. What is meant by "independence" in this context? Instead of treating the question mathematically and formally, we will take a less formal, more pragmatic view. Readers equipped with the necessary mathematical and statistical background should certainly consult the more formal literature. An excellent place to begin is in

Naus (1975), for a summary of the literature and an excellent bibliography. Its approach makes it a suitable complement to this volume.

For our purposes, the errors in two copies of an item are independent if an error in one item *tells us nothing new* about the possibility and nature of an error in the other.

The only time duplication *fails* to detect an error is when *the same error occurs in both items.* If the errors are independent, such double errors will occur less frequently than if the two errors spring from the same source. Moreover, independence permits the use of powerful statistical techniques to estimate the detection power, and to design to any desired level of detection.

Actually, what we would really like is not independence, but *negative dependence.* Negative dependence means that when an error occurs in one item, there is *less than average likelihood* of the same error in the other. Unfortunately, we don't know how to produce such negative dependence, so the best we can hope for is simple independence.

DEPENDENCE

It isn't easy to give examples of independence, for everything tends to be related to everything else in an system. Or, put in terms of a general principle, we have the Strong Connection Law (Weinberg, 1975):

A system is a collection of parts, no *one* of which can be changed.

Rather than *hope for independence*, we should *search for dependence*, to protect ourselves from surprises.

What kind of dependence could lower the error detection power of repetition? In the case of counting chairs, having some clerk count twice would obviously produce correlated errors. Having a different person deliver a second count should be better, but numerous factors mitigate the desirable effects.

For instance, if the first clerk tells the

second--before the second count--what the first count
was, then the second clerk may be influenced towards
reaching the same value. Or, the first clerk might
give instructions to "help" the second, such as,
"Don't count the chairs over there. They're part of
another batch." If he's right, the values will more
likely be right, but if he's wrong, the errors will
be correlated.

The physical situation itself may lead to correlated errors, as when some chairs are hidden under a
pile of others. Knowing how many chairs there *should*
be--based on parts used or quantity ordered--will influence the counting. If the source of this knowledge
is subsequently used as a second source of the count,
serious dependencies will exist.

CHECKING THE CHECKING

The list of potential dependencies could go on
and on, and should act to curb the optimism of any
input designer. Before discussing strategies for
obtaining independence, we should pause and consider
how we would *recognize* independence if we achieve it.

When using conventional "verification" techniques,
there is no record of the duplicate keying--only a
presumed "verified" card. Some verifying machines
produce a notch in the card, but to our knowledge, no
existing machines can read the notch. Therefore, the
only check on this type of multiple keying error is a
gross comparison of error rates reaching the computer.

If duplicate keying has actually been done, the
amount of "verified" information caught as erroneous
in later processing stages should remain relatively
constant. Several studies indicate that roughly 10-
15% of errors slip through in this way (see, for
example, Minton, 1969). If the error rate for each
application is measured over time, sudden changes may
indicate an alteration in the independence assumptions.

For example, a client's keypunch staff knowingly
notched 2,000 blank cards and then punched them only
once, without verification. They explained, "We had
to do it. It was Friday afternoon. But we were *very*

careful." This clever scheme was detected through an unusually high error rate in that batch of cards--the only way it could be detected in a system that presents only one keyed value to the computer.

When the results of *both* keyings are presented to the computer, there is much more information for monitoring the design assumptions. In many applications, "unverified" (that is, unnotched) cards are inserted by a variety of official and unofficial procedures into batches of otherwise verified cards. Whether this is an accident, or laziness, or an official decision, such cards cannot be distinguished from verified ones. With duplicate recording, however, errors in these cards are detected just as in any other. Among other benefits is the ability to simplify manual procedures in the assurance that the computer can do the checking.

Can the duplicate recording system be "cheated"? Presumably one could have a machine or program automatically duplicate one field into another, thus "saving work" for someone. In such a case, the cheating would be discovered by an abnormally *low* rate of errors. Of course, if we don't plan to record system error-detecting performance, we *deserve* to be cheated.

OBTAINING INDEPENDENCE

Though dependencies can creep into any system of checking by duplication, there is usually some design strategy that moves in the direction of independence. In what follows, we present a variety of such strategies as they might apply to keying duplicate items from a single source document--still the most frequent design problem.

DIFFERENT PEOPLE

Two different operators will have a tendency to hear and/or see things in slightly different ways, and also to miskey in different patterns. These differences are the principal advantage of the "key verification" technique, and can also be used when duplicate

items are produced for computer input. In many cases,
this method of achieving independence has disadvantages in cost and dangerous paper-handling--as source
documents are moved from person to person--which might
actually increase error rates reaching the computer.

Moreover, different people do not necessarily
produce the independence we need. A poorly written
value of 23 might easily be read by both operators as
28, yet other methods used by a single operator could
lead to recognition of this ambiguity.

When the second operator can *see* the first one's
keyed value, independence is almost completely de-
stroyed. In many key verification systems, the "verifier" is shown the original value when there is dis-
agreement, and then asked to make a decision. In such
circumstances, the "verifier" will tend to do just
what the name implies--"verify" that the original was
indeed correct.

In total, then, there are a variety of circumstances that destroy the independence of different
operators, such as

> *similar "first glance" interpretation, especially
> when a premium is placed on keying rate, rather
> than on overall accuracy*

> *the "positive" implication of the name, "verif-
> ier," and other job factors tending to make
> "confirmation" of the first value more acceptable
> behavior*

> *extra work that "penalizes" a verifier who has to
> change an existing value, as by punching a new
> card to replace the ruined one*

> *the implied punishment of the first operator if
> too many errors are found by the second.*

INTERVENING ACTION

Among the many alternatives to different people
performing duplicate keying, one of the best is to
have the single operator repeat the value only *after
some other action*. In the telegraph system, the

code repetition comes after the remainder of the message has been keyed. In demand repetition, the prompting intervenes to break the operator's psychological set. In invariant repetition, however, the designer must interpose some other item between the duplicate values in order to achieve the same effect. A typical case would be

28 RHYTHMOMETERS 23

Hopefully, by the time RHYTHMOMETERS is done, the operator will no longer "remember" the 28 and will have to look once again at the source document to see 23, the correct value.

Hopefully, too, the operator can be trained not to look at the original number as keyed, but at the actual source. This effect may be accomplished on certain terminals by not permitting the operator to see the first amount until the second amount is keyed.

REVERSE KEYING

An old practice from the days of manual computing is to *reverse* the order of the digits or characters. We have never seen this practiced in a data entry environment, but the principle is sound. By forcing the operator to read the information in an unfamiliar way, we get greater likelihood of independent keying. Painters often view landscapes upside down to be sure they see the colors, rather than the colors they think should be there because of the object's familiarity. Of course, reading backwards may become just as familiar as reading forward, in which case we lose some of the advantage of this proposed method:

668 ORGANOPHONES 866

TRANSFORMATIONS

Reversal is a special case of the more general technique of reducing dependence by *transforming* the data to another representation. There are many instances of transformations in non-computer practice, as in the amounts written on checks. Some other examples:

    234 GLOCKENSPIELS TWO THREE FOUR

    17.2 ... SEVENTEEN POINT TWO

    28/6 ... JUNE 28TH

    2PM   ... 1400

Just about any transformation that forces the operator to take a careful second look will achieve the desired result.

ORDER OF MAGNITUDE

Dependence may be reduced if the operator must *set a limit*. This technique is used in check writing when we see "not good for over $1,000," or "two signatures required for over $500." For instance, in

    234.56 REBATE 240

the operator must compute mentally (which should be easy, but not too easy) the next higher "round tens" amount.

The order of magnitude check can be introduced in a variety of ways. For instance, the operator can be asked to append an "L" for "large order," "M" for "moderately large order," "S" for "unusually small order," and nothing at all for orders in the normal range, as in

    668 ORGANOPHONES L

    234 GLOCKENSPIELS

    2   CLAVICITHERNS S

The *absence* of a letter after GLOCKENSPIELS may indicate that the large amount, 234, is in error.

IMPLICIT REPETITION

At times, order of magnitude information may be just lying around in other parts of the message, or in the customer record or product record. The same principle of repetition is in effect, but with the added advantages of much less dependence likely and no extra keying. Indeed, many of the good old standby checking techniques are precisely ways of checking a quantity, at least roughly, with explicit repetition of the same data item. Some examples are the following:

a total of all quantities in a group

a "hash" total of all numeric items on a document

a limit check for reasonable amounts in the product record, or in a table for a product category

a quantity-times-price calculation giving money amount reasonableness checks

plausability with respect to other criteria in data bank, such as, what type of customer is buying this quantity? Is he normally a big (or small) buyer? How much did he buy last time, or this year?

comparison of a payment with an amount billed, under the assumption that these will be identical in a great majority of cases, in certain systems.

Finally, we musn't fail to consider the possibility of no repetition at all. In some non-critical data collections, we can eliminate repetition on some or all input quantities. Many applications, for example, do not "verify" descriptive fields. This approach assumes that computers won't *ever* do anything with these fields except store them and copy them to output--where human beings will be able to apply their considerable powers of error detection and correction.

Be careful, though! "Never" is a long time. Watch out for these fields later on, when someone changes a system.

LET THEM THINK

In order to gain independence, all the suggested methods (except "verification") require the operator to break at least one pattern of thought and start another. Perhaps this difference accounts for the popularity of "verfication" among systems designers who consider keypunchers to be mindless automata.

Strangely, these same designers shrug their shoulders and say, "I told you so," when an operator keys 238.76 as 832.76. "Look," they add with haughty superiority, "any fool could see that this amount is too large for this transaction!"

There is a moral in this, worth setting down explicitly:

IF YOU WANT PEOPLE TO THINK, GIVE THEM A CHANCE

To start with, every data entry system should have some sort of "???" procedure--a way for the operator to escape from an overly rigid design, based merely on *intuition* that something is wrong. Such escape mechanisms grow naturally in most data entry departments, but get harder and harder to develop as the procedures get more automatic.

Note well that the *best* input systems do not attempt to prevent *all* errors--information theory says that's impossible anyway. Well-designed systems attempt to *limit the consequences* of error, which is a more appropriate objective. There really is *no* excuse for a computer system that bills a homeowner $132,192 for a month's worth of electricity. In particular, there is no excuse of the form, "It was a keypunch error." Anything that far out of line rests squarely on the shoulders of the *designer*--the one who thinks keypunchers are mindless, and designs that way.

In the end, what we are trying to accomplish is the kind of *reasonableness* the owner of the one-person business used to have. We'll know our designers have become professionals when their input system says, in response to some outlandish input:

36 CASES OF BOURBON? THIRTY-SIX?
WHY, I CAN'T REMEMBER WHEN HIRAM WALKER
EVER ORDERED THAT MUCH OF ANY WHISKEY.
HOW ABOUT CHECKING THAT AND CONFIRMING
THE QUANTITY. PERHAPS HE MEANT 36 BOTTLES.

TRIPLICATION

If we haven't thought carefully about designing to functional specifications, rather than to some abstract generalized idea of "efficiency," the idea of triplication (or even further multiplication) of data elements might seem outrageous. We see now, however, that it could have application whenever:

> *the volume of transactions involving the element is low, such as once a day or once an hour*
>
> *incorrect use of the number would be critical, such as mortal danger, scandal, crashing of a rocket, breakdown of a process being controlled.*

CORRECTION POSSIBILITIES

Many computer specialists automatically assume that triplication, such as

234 234 BROWN-SWISS/CHAROLAIS 234

4/3/5 ... MAR 4 75 ...750304

is distinct from duplication in the property of allowing *correction* based on a two-out-of-three majority logic. This possibility is not, however, generally applicable. Just as for detection, full correction power holds true only for cases where the error sources are "random" (such as pressing one wrong key once by accident) or otherwise independent of one another. It does not hold true for *systematic* repetition of errors due to human misunderstanding, machine error, program bugs, or simply human bias away from randomness in making errors.

PATTERNS OF HUMAN ERROR

Psychologists know that human beings demonstrate a *pattern* in their errors (ref: Campbell, 1958). Patterns exist within each person, and certain patterns

are common across large numbers of people. For instance, if we give keying exercises involving such a
number as 6623546 buried among other similar items,
we will find a large number of people converting this
number into 6623456--essentially "correcting" the
sequence.

Some of the typical tendencies toward non-random
errors in a keying situation are:

*abbreviation, simplification, condensation, loss
of detail, such as, leaving out an element, com-
bining two elements into one*

*loss of middle parts of the element, such as con-
verting 3478978564 into 3478564, or dropping elements in the middle of a list*

*closure, or filling in gaps, such as giving a
value to a missing element*

*creating symmetry, such as filling in one line
item to match the pattern of a preceeding one*

*bias toward the center, as in bringing "extreme"
values more toward the "norm"*

*assimilation to prior input, or to an expected
input*

Designers interested in more detail should consult Campbell's survey. Another source with a different perspective is the Bell System's *Common Language
Coding Guide*, which is not yet, unfortunately, available to the general design community. Some additional
insights from this source are given in terms of characteristics of the code user (described as "he,", in
spite of the fact that the majority of code users are
"she"):

*He is a creature of verbal habits. If a code is
difficult for him to verbalize, it is difficult
for him to remember and work with.*

*Probably related to his tendency to subvocalize
is the fact that he makes more errors in codes
drawn from acoustically similar vocabularies than
in codes from acoustically dissimilar vocabularies.*

Rudimentary aspects of his past still plague him in this age of electronics communication. He has more difficulty keying with his thumb, middle, and little fingers than with the index and ring fingers.

He evidences some consistency in the kinds of substitution errors he makes. His errors tend to be unidirectional, e.g., he generally substitutes a U for a V rather than a V for a U.

He tends to make his errors at the end of a short code, or just to the right of center in longer codes. Without special training or practice, he tends to make more errors with certain letters than with others--whether the letters are presented visually or aurally.

Good code design, or the use of natural materials instead of codes, can help reduce the number of errors a repetition system has to detect and correct. But there will always be some bias away from "randomness," so error correction schemes based on independence will never work quite as well as theoretically possible.

For instance, if a source telephone number is

687-1243

the tendency to "restore" sequence will make it quite likely we will receive, as our triple values,

687-1234   687-1243   687-1234

or

678-1234   687-1243   678-1234

In these cases, the matching of first and third values would lead our correction scheme to choose incorrect values.

Put another way, triplication will certainly allow correction of all single errors, but the frequency of single errors may be lower than expected on the basis of randomness. Furthermore, the frequency of *double* errors which are, in fact, the *same* error repeated will be higher than "random." Triplication-correction-by-majority will cause such items to be "corrected" to the wrong value, yet our guard will be lowered by the security of "automatic correction."

EXAMPLE: SCORING SPORTING EVENTS

In spite of all criticism, high levels of redundancy can prove most effective. One of the authors (Gilb) observed the data input terminal system used for collecting results from international figure skating competitions. The Skating Union rules require double keying, even for the apparently simple data collection procedure of gathering 9 two-digit numbers every 6 minutes. Here, accuracy is extremely important--at least if you think figure skating is important. Why bother scoring at all if it's not accurate? Speed of entry, on the other hand, is not too critical, as long as the 9 numbers are gathered before the next set is available 6 minutes later.

The system in use (Unidata, COBOL, Copenhagen, 1975, European Championship) was a nice match to these functional requirements, and did not blindly follow techniques conceived in other situations. Two separate operators keyed the results called out by the judges on separate visual display terminals on-line to the same computer, which could then compare inputs.

One observed case was this:

JUDGE	*1*	*2*	*3*	*4*	*5*	*6*	*7*	*8*	*9*
$SCORE_1$	56	57	56	57	58	58	54	56	55
$SCORE_2$	56	57	56	57	58	56	56	55	55

Yes, even in this simple task they did manage to key in errors, just like ordinary human beings. Because of the repetition, however, the errors were caught and corrected before they were allowed to affect the official lists.

The redundancy in this system is enormous. First, there is redundancy at the source, with nine judges providing protection against errors in "judging." Then there is redundancy in keying, with two (or more) separate operators. Finally, because the scores are called out loud, many spectators and the judges themselves can participate in checking the displayed results of the keying. In fact, the redundancy here approaches that found in biological systems, where reliable performance in the face of possible error means life or death.

UNDERSTANDABILITY

In some ways, the scoring example illustrates an extreme in redundancy and independence. The number of judges, terminal operators, and spectators could be increased to achieve almost any level of accuracy required by the rules or the importance of the outcome. It also illustrates another important design principle for "public" systems--understandability. More sophisticated systems could no doubt be devised, but would the officials understand what is going on? Would they get a good intuitive feel for the reliability of the method?

The same sort of understandability is needed, for example, in voting systems, systems which control dangerous machines, medical systems, and systems in which there might be danger of insiders manipulating the system to their personal advantage.

COMPRESSED DUPLICATION--CHECK DIGITS

Check digit schemes are well known in computing, so we won't make a complete recap here. Readers not familiar with the basic concepts of check digits might see Anderson, Hendershot, and Schoonmaker (1974). Some newer concepts may be found in Brown (1974). Brown also explores some correction possibilities using decimal check digits, a subject first raised by Weinberg (1961).

PARTIAL VERSUS FULL DUPLICATION

A simple "check digit" scheme would
Add the digits in the number to be checked.
Divide the sum by 10 and take the remainder,

which reduces the sum to a single digit. (This is called a modulus-10 method.)

Append the digit obtained in this way to the original number, which makes the new number "self-checking."

For instance, the unchecked number 743 would become the self-checked number 7434. The sum, 7 + 4 + 3 equals 14, which yields 4 as a remainder when divided by 10. Because the sum incorporates some information from each digit, we are, in effect, duplicating information. In contrast to full duplication, such as

743   743

the check digit is more compressed. Yet both share a number of properties:

The checking information is derived from the item alone, with no reference to other sources.

All parts of the element are somehow involved in the checking information, so that there is some protection for every part.

The method of deriving the checking information is systematic and unique--the same for all items and at all times.

They are essentially error detecting schemes, which require supplementary information if correction of detected errors is required.

There are, however, many important contrasts between the two methods:

COMPRESSED DUPLICATION	STRAIGHT DUPLICATION
fewer symbols to key	*fewer symbols to write*
more effort to create the redundancy--usually requiring machines	*simple on-the-spot creation of the redundancy by humans*
more complex error-detection algorithms	*simple human and computer error-detection using comparison*
more difficult to perform correction, for	*several types of correction possible--wrong char-*

COMPRESSED DUPLICATION	STRAIGHT DUPLICATION
it is hard to know which character is wrong	*acter can be identified by comparison; correct answer is probably one of only two alternatives; choice can often be made by validity check using files, tables, or algorithms*
detection of some classes of error is more convenient, for the detection mechanism is self-contained and standard, often built into simple hardware, and available in several variations	*cannot be "focussed" on one category of error*
normally convenient only for stable, predictable, numeric identifiers	*easily applied to all data types--alphabetic, quantities, dates*

DO THEY WORK?

In comparing alternative checking systems, the designer must not be trapped into *assuming* that a system will work just because someone says it will. We have just seen that *understandability* is an important attribute of checking systems. Unfortunately, "self-checking" numbers are sadly lacking in this property, and have consequently surprised more than one gullible designer.

For example, Alan Taylor (1975) reported the sad fate of the modulus-10 check-digit system used at the Pennsylvania Bureau of Sales and Use Tax. A 7-digit number was made "self-checking" by the following method:

The first digit was multiplied by a "weight" of 7.

The second digit was multiplied by a "weight" of 6.

The third through seventh digits were multiplied by weights of 5, 4, 3, 2, and 1, respectively.

These weighted values were summed.

The sum was divided by 10 to get the remainder, a single digit.

This digit was complemented (subtracted from 10) to obtain the check digit to be appended.

For example, the number 1211111 would produce 1 x 7 + 2 x 6 + 1 x 5 + 1 x 4 + 1 x 3 + 1 x 2 + 1 x 1 as the sum, 34. The remainder on division by 10 is 4, which complemented gives a check digit of 6. The checked number is therefore 12111116.

For some reason, the Pennsylvanians believed this form of compressed repetition would

detect all single digit replacements

detect all transpositions of adjacent digits

The reader may wish to test the understandability of this system by seeing how long it takes to demonstrate that this "self-checking" scheme has *neither* of these commendable properties.

Taylor then presented an alternative system, said to be in use by a German book club in Darmstadt and "doubtless other places." This method uses weights of (2, 1, 2, 1, 2, 1, 2), but performed the summation in a different way. Each product is reduced to a single digit by the ancient technique of "casting out nines"-- effectively giving the product modulo 9. Then the sum is computed and (evidently) taken modulo 10.

DO THEY REALLY WORK?

A few weeks later, somebody informed Taylor that this method was known not to detect transpositions of 9 and 0. And so it went, with letters and new columns appearing for several months. Finally, a Babson College professor, Magdy Riskalla, informed Taylor that a better approach to "self-checking" numbers was to *examine the properties* of any proposed system. Certain number pairs permitted by the system might be too

"close"--so that one could easily be corrupted into
the other. Starting with a list of such weaknesses,
the designer could produce a new system by not using
one member of a "close" pair. The numbers would never
be issued at all, so the weakness of the old system
would never become manifest.

Riskalla's proposal is, in fact, a sound one, and
has been tested in use since the 1950's. Unfortunately, it still has the drawback of not being understandable to ordinary people. In one installation, the
forbidden code combinations were put into circulation
several years after the original study--when extra
numbers were needed to handle growth. The statistic-
ian who performed the original analysis was not only
gone, but also his very existence was forgotten.

The Pennsylvania and Darmstadt systems give additional evidence that self-checking number systems
suffer from their esoteric origins. The Pennsylvania
system is an inferior variant of IBM's old modulus-10
method (Form No. G24-1057) and the Darmstadt system is
an inferior variant of IBM's old modulus-11 system
(Form No. G24-1022). These methods have evidently
been transmitted through an oral tradition from one
generation of designers to another, with slight corr-
uptions being introduced from time to time by people
incapable of making the necessary analyses. Or, by
people who couldn't stand to use a method "not invented here."

The moral is clear. *Every* detection or correction scheme has weaknesses. *Every* designer is inclined
to have a lover's blindness to the weaknesses of "his"
scheme. Therefore, if the scheme is too complicated
for ordinary people to understand rather easily, we
are exposed to such dangers as

> *the system not working as promised, but everybody
> being unaware of the deficiency*
>
> *everybody being aware, but everybody also being
> afraid to change the system*
>
> *the system working well, but someone changing it
> because nobody understands why it works well*

In other words, you should observe the following maxims when designing input checking:

KEEP IT SIMPLE, BUT
DON'T BET YOUR ENTIRE SYSTEM ON ONE FORM OF DEFENSE.

DUPLICATION PLUS CHECK DIGITS

One simple form of multiple defense uses check digits and duplication in concert to provide the correction power each lacks when used singly. If we have a check digit scheme that detects all single digit errors, duplication of the checked identifier provides *correction* of all such errors. For instance, the "Darmstadt" method applied to the number 1230 gives a check digit of 8, or a self-checking number of 12308.

If an operator keys

12308   12348

the computer will discover that the second number doesn't check. Because the first number does check, it can be taken as the correct value--an assumption that works unless there are multiple errors. Therefore, this simple scheme gives (at least) automatic correction of all single digit errors. To compute the full corrective power, we would have to simulate, or carry out a rather difficult mathematical analysis. Even with its single-digit corrective power, however, it's an excellent example of the power of multiple defenses.

THE RELATION BETWEEN REPETITION AND OTHER CONTROLS

On the subject of multiple defenses, perceptive designers often ask if duplication is needed when checks exist at the level of a batch of messages.

A BATCH SYSTEM

Consider a simplified batch input, designed in two alternative modes:

UNDUPLICATED	*DUPLICATED*
20 bank	20 bank 20
30 post	30 post 30
100 cash	100 cash 10
20 post	20 post 20
10 check	10 check 10
90 sum	90 sum 90

The amounts (in an actual system there would be more of them, from 20 to 200, typically) are controlled by means of the batch total checksum. Without the duplication, we have no choice but to wait for the sum before taking any action on the error, or even knowing it exists. When we do find a discrepancy in the check sum, we have another rather different and difficult task of locating the item in error.

The bigger the batch, the more likely it is to contain an error, and yet the more difficult it is to find the error. In computing the cost of the two systems, we must be sure to consider not just initial keying time, but the time and trouble taken to correct errors. Once we have added this into the batch side of the ledger, we often find that "redundant" punching is cheaper.

With the duplicated field, in a batch environment, our computer can tell

that there is an error somewhere

which item is likely to be in error

what the correction is likely to be

You can verify for yourself that this is possible with a reasonably small amount of programming. Naturally, we also have to provide for those cases in which *multiple* errors make it impossible to correct automatically, but notice how the combination of checksum and double entry makes it less likely that some *systematic* human error will penetrate our system unnoticed.

THE SAME SYSTEM ON-LINE

When keying on-line, or even to reasonably intelligent terminals, an immediate reaction to the erroneous line is possible, without waiting for the entire batch to be entered. The correction here is cheaper and more reliable, because the source document is still available.

On the other hand, we may still wish to keep the checksum on the batch, to give a second level of protection. We can view the checksum as checking the duplication process, or vice versa. Those who doubt the power of this combined technique should consider the several hundred years of "double entry bookkeeping" --still in common use, even in computer systems.

A LESSON FOR DESIGNERS

The moral is clear and familiar. When designing input systems, consideration must be given to the cost and ease of actually locating and correcting errors. Because errors are "infrequent," we may assume that their cost is insignificant, as long as they are detected and corrected in "some way or another."

It would do input designers a world of good to hang around a data preparation area for a few days, getting involved in the correction process when the batch totals don't match. Not too involved, though, so that they may retain enough perspective to make an estimate of what such a procedure costs the organization. Then they will realize that it is not sufficient to "have some way of detecting and correcting the error." Whatever way is used--whether or not the computer is involved--must be as responsive to the user's objectives as any other factor in the design.

In practice, responsiveness may dictate a variety of dection and correction methods in parallel or, rather, in harmony. Multiple methods will increase the probability of error *detection*, simplify the process of error *location*, and will aid both human and automatic *correction*.

And, lest you think this is a *new* lesson for computer people, we'd like to repeat the lesson in the words of Charles Babbage, the first computer designer, first published in 1864 (yes, *eighteen* sixty-four) but first remarked at least as early as 1827:

> *One element in the price of every article is the cost of its verification.*

EXTRA CORRECTION ABILITY

Having previously warned against the possibility of getting *less* correction ability than we might expect from majority rule, we should also observe that we can sometimes get more. For example, one of the repeated values may be clearly impossible, as in

28 MAR 1979   82 MAR 1979

It might not be worth programming the computer for this case, but a human operator looking at both values, has a very high probability of choosing the correct one.

Human operators can correct the above situation because they carry extra information about the actual system being modeled by the information system. Such extra information creates a potential for correction where, on the surface, only detection is possible. Humans can use this potential without special programming--one major reason we want to let them think. But, in many cases, rather simple computer programming can also accomplish surprising feats of correction.

One of our clients implemented the following simple but effective correction scheme in a receivables application. Payment amount is keyed twice, in the form

payment-1 account-number other-info payment-2

A standard-sized group of amounts is batch-totaled. If any pair of amounts fails to agree, both are compared with the latest billed amount. If one matches, it is presumed correct and the posting made.

Matching the billed amount corrects a great

majority of the erroneous keyings. Any unmatched
transaction is stacked in memory. When the batch sum
arrives and only one record is in the stack, the program chooses either value that makes the total come
out right. A large percentage of the remaining errors
are corrected in this step.

All corrective actions are logged for later statistical analyses. Records not correctable are reported for manual intervention. If the cost is justified, the designers can adjust the level of manual
intervention to be almost as low as desired. The principal adjustment is reducing the size of the batch for
totaling to produce fewer cases for manual adjustment.
Although batch totaling must be a manual operation, it
is much cheaper and more predictable than after-the-
fact correction.

What this example, and others like it, demonstrate is another rule for designers:

LOOK FOR, OR PROVIDE, A LITTLE EXTRA INFORMATION

A QUANTITATIVE EXAMPLE: LETTER SORTING

An item in *Computing Europe* (17 April 1975) discusses
the problems of mail sorting in the US Post Office.
In this application, the only item keyed is, essentially, a "Zip Code," or 5-digit number assigned by
the post office as a sorting key. (Let us put aside,
for now, the adequacy of this item design, and many
other factors, and make a rough model of the sorting
room of a post office.)

IN THE SORTING ROOM

Machines are provided to do all handling of the
letters. The machines orient the letters for reading
and pass them to reading stations manned by human operators. The operator has merely to read the address
and key the zip code. Using the keyed information,
the machines then dispatch each letter to an appropriate bin for distribution to other post offices.

The letters "fly by" the operator at the rate of

one per second. Conditions being what they are in this application, 9.1% of the letters handled this way are miskeyed by the operator. The machines themselves missort 1.8%, and 3.1% are mishandled in some way even after correct sorting. These figures may be important in the design, because they set a minimal standard for the sorting procedure. It will be diminishingly useful to sort more accurately if the letters are to be mishandled anyway.

The initial reaction of the management to poor sorting accuracy was to speed up the machines from 50 to 60 letters per minute. As explained in the article, "the speed was increased because it was believed that the gain in productivity would more than offset the additional errors that would probably result." It would be hard to imagine a more misguided policy, for we can predict that when people are treated inhumanly, they won't react idly.

When you tell a worker that you really don't care how accurately he works, but only how fast, this mistaken notion of "productivity" is bound to demoralize the workers and produce less productivity in the end.

According to the article, the workers responded by "dumping" the mail--that is. keying letters to bins which receive *another* sort.

AN ALTERNATIVE DESIGN

Let's assume that the workers are not subject to fatigue, and are motivated to help management. Let's further, for the sake of argument, assume that the workers get $7.20 per hour, and the machines run at 60 letters per minute, or 3600 per hour. Not even allowing for breaks (and of course, nobody could work at a job like this without frequent and refreshing breaks), this comes to a keying cost of $.002 per letter. But such a cost analysis doesn't take into account the cost of *correcting* for missorted letters--a cost which may well involve a lot more than $.002 per letter, when all has been considered.

Rather than trying to estimate the cost of correcting a miskeyed letter, let's evaluate an alternative design based on "duplicate" keying. Then we can see what the correction cost would have to be for the two methods to be equally costly.

Suppose our alternative system passes the letter from the first keystation to a second without sorting, but retaining the keyed information. A second operator rekeys the zip code, and if the codes keyed are identical, the letter is sorted immediately. If not, the letter moves on to a *third* station, perhaps fed by several streams, where the zip code is keyed one more time. If the keying here agrees with one of the two previous keyings, the letter is sorted according to majority logic. If not, it is handled manually.

SENSITIVITY TO ERROR COST

If we make some rough assumptions of independence of errors, we can see that with a miskeying rate of 9.1%, 174 out of 1000 letters will have one or more wrong zip codes keyed, and thus will pass to the third stage. 8 of these will have *both* previous keyings wrong, and thus cannot be accepted correctly in any case. Of the others, about 151 will be acceptable by majority logic, so that 15 letters will have to be sorted by hand in some way. In exchange for this reduced manual handling we have paid with 2174 keyings instead of 1000.

What would the cost of manual handling have to be to break even?

The cost of method 1, C_1, is given by

$$C_1 = .002 \times 1000 + 91 \times M$$

where M is the unknown cost of manual handling. We assume that M is the same for this operation and for the operation where the missorting is spotted in the keying process itself. Because late-detected errors are generally much more costly than those detected early, this is a *very* conservative assumption.

The cost of method 2, C_2, is given by

$$C_2 = .002 \times 2174 + 15 \times M$$

so the breakeven value of M may be calculated to be that for which C_1 and C_2 are equal. This turns out to

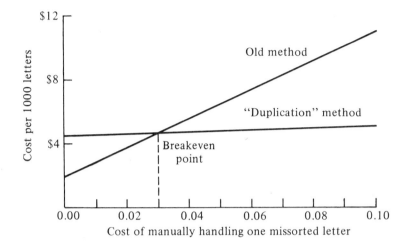

Figure 5.2   Sensitivity of two designs to cost of error handling.

be about $.03 per letter, as indicated by the crossing of lines in Figure 5.2. So, if the cost of manual handling (M) exceeds 3 cents, the repetition method should save money in the overall process.

ALTERNATIVES

The above calculations are rough, and conservative on several counts. First of all, in a real system we would want to consider whether *all* zip codes should be duplicated. First class mail might get this treatment, but mass mailings might not deserve such attention. Computer printed or typed zip codes might be better processable by optical scanners, and might be given reduced rates to encourage clearly printed zip codes.

Using such concepts, we can focus attention on those cases most likely to be wrong or, if wrong, most likely to be critical. Selective duplication is likely to increase the profitability of this technique, with a small sacrifice in service. And, if the error

rate is small enough, return mailings may be the cheap-
est method of correction. Only a study of actual
costs should determine whether these are economical
solutions.

But raw economic calculations leave us unsatis-
fied. A proper design must also consider such factors
as:

> *the increased morale of the workforce that knows*
> *that reliability is important*
>
> *the increased service to the mail users*

Postal workers and postal customers seem to have
been forgotten up until now, in a narrow-minded attempt
to "reduce costs." A more humane system *would* probably turn out to be cheaper--although that's not the
fundamental reason for designing it that way.

Approximately 100,000,000,000 pieces of mail are
handled each year--not all of them through this system.
A more complete study of the effects of "redundancy"
could well be justified, but isn't likely to be made.
When most of the "cost" is borne by people who don't
realize it (the people who mail letters), we are unlikely to see such an approach.

Whether the situation in any "real" postoffice
fits this model, we can't say. Still, many other applications could benefit from considering the *correction cost* as part of the "productivity" cost. Someday
we may consider the *human costs* that can't be measured
in dollars and cents.

A SUMMARY OF EXPECTED ATTRIBUTES

The following is a simplified multidimensional view of
the normal attributes which the designer can expect
when specifying the technique of repetition. The
designer must calculate or otherwise estimate the more
accurate attributes for his particular implementation
in order to compare this option against other design
alternatives.

PRODUCTIVITY

On the face of it, repetition seems to *decrease* productivity by large factors. These factors are reduced, however, by such techniques as exceptional and demand repetition. In fact, repetition costs no more keying effort than the frequently used repetitive verification by two "independent" readings of the source document. Repetition is often more effective and less costly than this type of verification.

Furthermore, when full consideration is given to detection/location/correction as part of the cost of productivity, the net result may be arbitrarily greater. Careful studies must be done before dismissing duplication techniques based on gross productivity estimates. Indeed, when the main objective is productivity, one would do well to consider repetition quite early, along with other error-correcting and detecting techniques.

RELIABILITY

Repeated codes must have higher reliability to justify their use, but the precise amount of increase depends on numerous factors including independence of errors, technique used, practice by operators, and the nature of the errors in the first instance. Many of these factors are discussed in detail in the chapter.

PORTABILITY

There is very little to prevent repetition techniques from being completely portable, unless we are moving "down" in hardware. For instance, if we move to a card version of an entry system that has been designed around records longer than 80 characters, we may find it impossible to squeeze the record size without eliminating repetition. While this situation may be infrequent, there are instances in which small stations may have lesser equipment and yet have to be compatable with larger ones.

If such downward movement is anticipated, the designer can consider the spectrum of devices to which the system might be moved, to determine the least common denominator of record size and character set. If this least common denominator is unsatisfactory for some other reason, then the designer will have to settle for less than full portability--or else upgrade the available devices.

Otherwise, there is a general rule relating portability and error-handling. The higher the error-handling reliability designed into the system, the more portable it will be. Because more information is available for error-handling, the staff will get into effective operation more quickly after the changeover. Also, if keying errors increase temporarily when new keying equipment is introduced (as is often observed) the impact will be reduced because of the better checking, and the transition will present one less headache.

IMPLEMENTATION EASE

For straight duplication, no form changes and few procedural changes should be necessary. Only the keying operator need change procedure. Additional programming for error detection is trivial, but can become more involved if the repetition is used as the basis for error correction.

Under variants of straight duplication, operator training may increase slightly, and additional programming may be required. Generally, however, more understandable methods are easier to implement. As long as the designers take time to apply some simple reasoning to their design alternatives, there shouldn't be any "surprises"--global effects on the rest of the application in unforseen places.

HARDWARE RESOURCES

Repetition schemes require no special hardware. The number of keying stations and capacity of transmission lines can be readily calculated on the basis of average keying effort, exception frequencies, and other design parameters. Our experience has never shown an increase in needed capacity, though decreases can result from elimination of "verification." Error detection logic has no measurable influence on CPU load. Attempts at automatic correction, however, should be estimated in advance, especially if they lead to consideration of many possible correction hypotheses.

SECURITY

Repeated codes are, of course, easier to *read* when taking an unauthorized glance. On the other hand, they are more difficult to *alter*, as is demonstrated by the conventional bank check--on which the two forms of the amount are hard to alter simultaneously in the same manner.

EXTENDABILITY

Repetition places no particular restriction on extension of input language or devices. When repeated message parts are separated to achieve independence, it may be difficult to find the place to add new parts in an unambiguous manner. On the other hand, the more to the message, the more independence we can anticipate when repeating parts, so extending may actually improve error detection performance.

DESIGN EXERCISES

1. Repeat Exercise 1 of Chapter 4 (page 109) using repetition techniques where applicable to increase conformity to quality requirements. Discuss how these techniques affected the performance of other aspects of the design, or if they did not, why not.

2. Show how to simulate demand repetition as described in the text. Be sure to include learning effects in your model.

3. List at least 5 ways in which the dual-entry scoring system of the skating competition might not be as error-resistant as we would like. Then list a technique for each by which performance may be restored.

4. In some data preparation with which you are familiar, make a study to determine the true overall cost of handling errors. Be sure to trace the effects of the errors to their ultimate resolution. Does this cost justify looking into methods of handling errors earlier and more efficiently? What is the overall contribution to (or, really, subtraction from) productivity of this error cost?

5. And old and well-tried method of obtaining systematic redundancy in a fixed set of codes is to use only multiples of a certain number, usually prime. One advantage of these systems is the ease with which we can study their properties using mathematical analysis. For instance, a system using multiples of 11 could never be cracked by a single digit substitution, as can be proved from an examination of the divisibility by 11 of simple powers of 10. Examine some other numbers, besides 11, which can be used in this way, and compare advantages and disadvantages of each. At what point does this method approach duplicate keying?

Chapter VI

Checkwords

This the Banker suggested, and offered for hire
(On moderate terms), or for sale,
Two excellent Policies, one Against Fire,
And one Against Damage from Hail.

The Hunting of the Snark, Fit the First

In the preceding chapter, we saw, in its simplest form, the principle that "extra" or "redundant" information need not be extra or redundant at all, in the sense of helping to achieve the system design criteria. Added information "insured" the messages against error. Moreover, redundant messages could be *self*-correcting-- roughly speaking, correctable without making reference to information outside of the message.

In this chapter, we examine a way of obtaining error detection and correction by comparing information outside of the message with redundant information within the message--the "checkword" (Gilb, 1973). Although the checkword may seem to be buying a second insurance policy, there are advantages to being protected Against both Fire and Hail--or Against any two

Independent Threats to system data integrity. Checkword techniques offer this extra protection "on moderate terms."

METHODS OF FINDING STORED DATA

In designing retrieval methods, we usually seek *rapid
retrieval* and *flexibility*. *Reliability*, however,
stands ahead of either of these, for there's no sense
getting information quickly and easily if it's the
wrong information.

POINTERS AND KEYS

If the designer has only machines to consider,
the fastest method of retrieval is a *pointer*--an internally generated computer symbol that is, in effect,
the physical address of the information. The pointer
is saved when the information is put away and recalled
whenever the computer needs that information.

There are two big disadvantages to pointers:

*They become invalid if information is moved, and
so limit the system's flexibility in managing its
storage facilities.*

*They are seldom in a form well suited to human
memory, and thus cannot be used successfully outside the computer.*

These disadvantages are removed by the use of
keys--unique symbols assigned to each stored entity.
A social security number is supposed to be a key--a
symbol attached to each person, and never given to two
people. A catalog number is a key to information
about a particular item in stock. A license number is
a key to information about a particular automobile.

Obviously, a social security number cannot generally be used as the physical address of a person's
record in a computing system. Instead, an index must
be created relating each social security number to its
corresponding address--that is, relating each key to
its pointer. Searching this index (or making an

equivalent transformation) slows down retrieval, but allows the file design to be independent of the particular arrangement of records. If a record must be moved, the social security number need not be changed, but only an entry in the index.

Keeping one social security number for life is a convenience for the person who has to remember it. Having no social security number to remember would be even more convenient, but not for the computer. Without the social security number--a key--computer systems would need more than a simple index search to retrieve any record.

Computer mythology dies hard. One of the oldest myths is that a key lets the computer retrieve any record with a simple index search. For that myth to be true:

All keys have to be entered with zero probability of error.

All users of a key have to be perfectly honest.

Where but in design "mythodology" are these true for *any* key?

IDENTIFIERS

Perhaps system designers should forget about keys and think in terms of *identifiers*--items of information *tending* to identify other items of information. Then, instead of concocting ways to coerce people into using keys, they could concentrate on the processes to retrieve information using the natural identifiers that already exist.

The retrieval process involving identifiers can be characterized like this:

1. Use the identifier to obtain a pointer to some information.

2. Check that the information addressed is that which is sought.

3. If the information is incorrect, either inform the user that the information cannot be retrieved or attempt retrieval again by incorporating more information from the input.

In other words, the identifier is a first approximation--a guide to starting the process of retrieving information. With this generalized concept of retrieval, we can design systems for environments in which:

identifiers cannot be guaranteed unique, such as with names or descriptions

identifiers may be entered in error

some users may be dishonest.

CHECKWORDS

We may define an identifier as

message data used in trying to find a record in a file

Because that trial may prove unsuccessful, the retrieval process may have to incorporate other information. We may define a *checkword* as

message data available for comparison with record content to determine the probability that the system has found the record we intended to find

Like the check digit or the password, the checkword is "redundant" information. That is, checkwords are useless when we can be 100% sure that the identifier will locate the right information, all the right information, and nothing but the right information. The only time that fortunate situation *might* prevail is when using internal pointers. In all other cases, checkwords are potentially useful, as in the following examples:

EXAMPLE	EXPLANATION
241240 GILB	*Personal employee identification number, with first four characters of last name used as checkword.*
Q3.W4 INTGST	*Book identified by call number, with condensed title used as*

EXAMPLE	EXPLANATION
Q3.W4 WEIN	*checkword--first 3 characters of first significant word, followed by first character of each other significant word. In this case, title is An INTroduction to General Systems Thinking, by WEINberg, which could be used as an additional checkword, as in the previous example.*
197-2301-4 137NW	*Legal property code identifier, with checkword created from numeric part of street address and city quadrant.*
1410 KOLBOTN	*Postal code identifier (zip code in USA) with place name used as checkword. Because there are often duplicate place names (Lincoln, NE and Lincoln, CA), the name makes a poor identif- ier, but can be used as a good checkword because there will rarely (if ever) be two ident- ical place names within the same postal code.*
68505 LINCOLN	
95648 LINCOLN	

As these examples indicate, a good identifier will fetch a unique, correct record *most of the time.* A good checkword will be able to confirm this selec- tion, most of the time, and helps in making another selection if the original one is not confirmed. It doesn't matter *why* the identifier fails. It could be a damaged unique identifier or one that was inherently ambiguous. The checkword operates equally well in either case.

CHECKWORD CHARACTERISTICS

The following paragraphs present a sampling of the choices available to the designer of a checkword scheme, along with some general considerations under- lying those choices.

SOURCE

Sources of checkwords are characterized by one or more of the following principles:

The checkword may be "picked up" from existing material in the text of a source document.

When there is no source document--as with telephone orders or factory-floor systems--the checkword can be picked up from some natural part of the interaction protocol.

The person who originally produces the source of the checkword need not be aware of it as a checkword.

If no source is available in all messages, alternative sources can be used.

For extra security, an identifier may have more than one checkword.

A single checkword can sometimes check two or more identifiers in one message.

Checkwords increase their power when used in conjunction with other error detection and correction methods.

We can usually find adequate checkwords in existing documents or procedures--even in existing keyed material. Some further examples of checkwords illustrate this point:

a telephone number printed on the company letterhead

part of a telephone number, such as the exchange only, or the last 4 digits only

a few letters extracted from a product description scribbled on an order alongside product code

the retail price, noted on the order by the salesman or customer

the street address on a tax return

part of a street address, such as the digits only, or the first three letters of the street name author's initials given with a book order

the date taken from an engineering drawing

CHECKWORDS AND CHECK DIGITS

Some of our clients are misled by the confusion in *names* between "checkword" and "check digit." Once the principle underlying their function is grasped, there should be no confusion between the two, because they are essentially *opposites:*

Check *digits* are a system for checking when *no memory is available*, and thus *must* be derivable from the identifier to be checked.

Check*words* take *full advantage of memory*, which means they should *never* be derivable from the identifier to be checked.

Let's consider an example to show why checkwords should never be derivable from the identifier. We want to invent a checking scheme for a personal ident- ification number, such as 319-31-6790. Suppose we extract the first digit of each subsequence, giving a "checkword" of 336. This is a *terrible* choice. All this amounts to is *partial duplication* of the number as keyed. As such, it will be less effective than even the simplest check *digit* scheme, for

It won't check 6 of the 9 digits *at all*.

It won't check errors in the initial digits if they occured between the source and the keying.

It won't check for misreading of a digit by the keying operator.

In short, it's a *bad* system of checking--neither a checkword nor a check digit.

Now let's contrast this poor choice with a check- word taken from the person's name--let's use the 2 or 3 initials. Under this system, in order for an error in the personal identification number to go undetected, two conditions are necessary:

1. The erroneous number would have to match some

record in the data bank.

2.   The name in that record would have to have exactly *the same initials as the proper person.*

DETECTION POWER

How likely is condition (1)? We don't know without knowing the manner in which the numbers were assigned, but suppose they were all multiples of 13. This method (see Exercise 5, page 152, of Chapter V) should catch 100% of single-digit errors and 100% of adjacent transpositions. These two types might account for, say, 99% of all errors in the application. This leaves 1% of the errors to be caught by the next line of defense, the checkword.

How likely is condition (2)? Again, an exact analysis would be cumbersome, and depend on many factors. If, however, we can assume that the identity code assignment is *independent* of the person's name, we can make a fair approximation. Not everyone has 3 initials, but assume so for simplicity. There are 26^3 different checkwords, from AAA to ZZZ. Not all combinations are equally likely, for QXQ might be rare and JFK rather frequent. So, instead of the full 17,576 combinations, we might effectively have 10,000.

To be *very* conservative in our estimate, let's make the effective number of combinations 1,000. In that case, there would be about 1 chance in 1,000 of getting a checkword match by accident. If the self-checking number misses only 1 out of 100, the *combination* of the two *independent* methods will miss no more than 1 out of 100,000--by very conservative estimates. If there is one *error* in every 10 identifiers (a fair estimate for keypunching), then 1 in 1,000,000 records will be retrieved erroneously in spite of the double line of defense. Actual performance could be considerably better, because of our conservatism in estimating.

If, however, the checkword is in *any* way dependent on the identification number itself, we can no longer make this estimate with assurance. That is why we want the two to be as independent as possible.

In this example, independence is likely to be achieved to a high degree because of such factors as:

One is numeric and the other is alphabetic, so a keying or handwriting bias is unlikely to affect both in the same way.

The operator isn't even aware that the two are related, so can't unconsciously force *a match.*

There is no connection between the choice of name and the choice of number (an assumption that won't be true of some alpha-to-numeric coding schemes).

The two items come from different parts of some source document so, for example, bad carbon copying is less likely to affect both.

In other words, the *one* thing that can destroy the relevance and validity of a checkword is the possibility of *deriving it from the identifier*. And that is the property that *defines* a check *digit*, so we should never confuse the two.

MULTIPLE CHECKWORDS

We can better appreciate the above argument by a glance at Figure 6.1. This Figure is the familiar

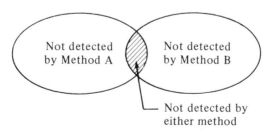

Figure 6.1   Error detection potential of two simultaneously applied methods of error detection.

Venn diagram. Each circle represents the set of all errors not detected by one of the methods, so the *overlapping* region is the errors not detected by *either* method. To minimize the number of undetected errors, we try to keep this overlap as small as possible, which is what we achieve by independence of the methods.

Another way to reduce the area of intersection is by creating a *third* method, which adds a third circle to the diagram, as shown in Figure 6.2.

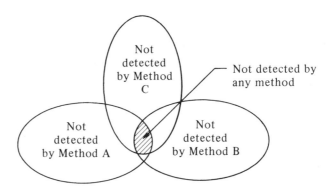

Figure 6.2   Error detection potential of three
             simultaneously applied methods of
             error detection.

We can choose the second checkword as the third detection method--perhaps taking the digits from the person's street address. This choice will probably be independent of the other two pieces of information. If there are, effectively, 1,000 street addresses, we would reduce the chance of an undetected error to 1 in 100,000,000. And remember, that is 1 in 100,000,000 *errors*, not messages.

In spite of this reasoning, multiple independent checkwords are extremely rare in our experience. Why? There are a variety of possible explanations:

At a certain point, the number of "false alarms"

coming from miskeyed checkwords starts to cost more than the extremely small fraction of errors penetrating the system.

There is, in any application, a certain finite chance of a complete blunder, such as the operator keying the name and address from one source document and the rest of the material from another. Such blunders limit our assumption of independence of errors, no matter what our checkword scheme. Because this probably happens at least once in 1,000,000 documents, it would become the dominant source of error, and additional effort spent on checkwords would not be profitable.

At a certain point, the extra keying (if there is extra keying) to get the checkwords costs more than the additional errors found, because the number of remaining errors is very small to start with.

ALTERNATIVE CHECKWORDS

Because checkwords are often derived from indicative information, it may not be possible to use a single method that works for all cases. For instance, the house number can't be used on such addresses as:

CHECKERBOARD SQUARE

WILDCAT LANE

RURAL FREE DELIVERY

On the other hand, it may not always be possible to get a "person's" initials, in such cases as:

GARBANZO INC.

WILLIAMSONS

SUPERMAN

In such cases, we may employ *alternative* checkwords, such as, a house number as an alternative to initials. This pair would be exceptionally simple to process, as they self-identify--house numbers being numeric and initials, alphabetic.

On the other, this simple set of alternatives might still be incomplete, for we could certainly have addresses such as:

```
WILLIAMSONS              GARBANZO, INC.
RURAL FREE DELIVERY      GARBANZO, IDAHO
PRARIE HOME, NEBRASKA
```

We should always provide a "clean-up" rule, to be sure a checkword can invariably be derived. Here, we could choose the first three letters of the name, or first *four*, to identify this kind of checkword by *length*.

One clean-up rule that must work is to have a special word meaning *no rule applies*--such as XXX. If cases such as the above are rare, and if the computer can also determine that no rule applies, then XXX will be an effective alternative checkword.

VARIANT CHECKWORDS

When there is great variation in the information from which the checkword is derived, the checking program may have to *accept* more than one checkword. For example, there may be spelling variations in a name, or a middle name may not always be given, or different operators may, in fact, apply a rule differently. If, for instance, we are to take the initial letters of the name, omitting "non-significant words," how would we derive a checkword from

MASON AND DIXON PTY LTD

Different operators could conceivably come up with MAD, MDP, MDL, and even MD.

Some such variation can be eliminated if the computer itself derives the checkword from the fully keyed information. Even then, alternatives must be allowed, as when the operator keys

MASON & DIXON PTY LTD

for the above example, which could generate additional variants, such as M&D.

LENGTH

Another consideration is the *size* of the checkword, for which a few guidelines can be listed:

There is no necessary maximum length for a checkword.

In practice, 2 to 4 characters are common and sufficient, and rarely does a checkword exceed 6 characters in length.

If the "natural" checkword can be longer than we need, permit the operator to enter the long word as an alternative form. For example, if the telephone number is used, but the "area code" is the same for most customers, eliminating the area code would save keystrokes. But if the operator does include the area code, by mistake or for comfort, the computer can recognize the extra length and eliminate it internally. The operator isn't burdened with more rules than a simple "punch the telephone number."

Frequently, terminating information can be dropped. If, for instance, we are using the first 3 letters of the first significant word of the title, plus the initial of each other significant word, we might get arbitrarily long checkwords, as from

EVERYTHING YOU ALWAYS WANTED TO KNOW ABOUT
SEX * BUT WERE AFRAID TO ASK

which could produce

EVEYAWTKAS*BWATA

Truncations after the first 6 characters would lessen keying and reduce the chance of ambiguity arising from the later, less significant parts of the title. In any case, the operator need not count characters, as long as enough are given to identify whatever record is being sought. Counting characters is error-prone, and to be avoided.

POSITION

Here are some guidelines for positioning the checkword:

In practice, the most common position for a checkword is close to the corresponding identifier--either immediately before or immediately after. In some applications, checkwords are determined in advance and placed side-by-side with the identifier, as in 12345-NYL on an order form.

In spite of this common practice, the strongest checking arises from independence. When identifier and checkword are side-by-side, they are subject to corruption by the same physical forces, such as smudging, coffee spills, defective carbon paper, or bumpy writing surface.

Unlike check digits, which historically had to be adjacent to the corresponding identifier, there is nothing sacred about the relative positions of checkword and identifier. If they are sufficiently self-identifying, we can permit them to appear in any place and in any order.

A checkword arising from some otherwise significant element--such as price or an address--should be placed in its "natural" position in the keying sequence.

Checkwords may be optionally omitted, under a variety of circumstances.

DEMAND CHECKWORDS

Checkwords can be given on *demand*, in interactive situations. The following annotated dialogue illustrates the method and some of its advantages:

INTERACTION	REMARKS
3 78965	*Ordering 3 of item 78965.*
	Item is found, no demand is made.
2 12345	*Ordering 2 of item 12345.*

INTERACTION	REMARKS
PLEASE GIVE A PRODUCT-NAME CHECK	*Item isn't found under 12345, so computer demands a checkword.*
BLT	*Operator derives BLT from BOLT. In this case, BOLT might have been better.*
UNABLE TO MAKE UNIQUE CHOICE--HELP! IS IT 72345 BELT, BLACK? OR 2345 BOLT-1/2"?	*BLT is not sufficiently explicit to resolve BELT and BOLT.*
21 2345 BOLT	*Operator now sees keying error (2 12345 for 21 2345) and corrects, giving checkword, just to be sure.*
TWENTY-ONE 2345 BOLT	*Confirmation.*
2 DRI 89002	*New transaction. Program accepts any sequence, and accepts checkword even if not demanded.*
TWO 98002 DRILL??	*Product number was wrong, but unique correction was possible using DRI as the checkword.*
24 55438	*Operator merely continues with next transaction if computer's "guess" is correct.*

CONTENT

Designers frequently have trouble deciding what goes into a checkword. Fortunately, the first principle of checkword design relieves some of the strain:

The content of the checkword is not supercritical, as it is being used to confirm, *rather than to* locate.

Additional principles may be given to aid the designer's choice of content:

Any combination of meaningful alphabetic, numeric, or special character information may be used. Because of the human use and origin of most check- words, alphabetic characters are most frequent.

If properly designed, a checkword can be used as an approximate sorting key--to gain an initial sort into coherent groups. In one case, a mail- ing code was used as a checkword, and mailing labels could then be sorted according to post office requirements using the checkword alone.

The checkword generally picks up somewhat more of the source document than input designs have trad- itionally done.

"Traditional" input design concentrated on reducing keystrokes to a minimum, and cramming as many codes as possible into 80 columns. In doing so, the designers eliminated the type of information humans use in mak- ing plausible corrections--thus rendering the operat- ors even more helpless to improve their performance.

Checkwords reverse this dehumanizing trend. Any information people might use in making corrections is a candidate for a checkword. In one instance, the checkword included the color of the source document, which helped identify its origin.

In designing checkwords, first make a list of the most plausible errors. Then figure out, or observe, how people would detect or correct each error using the source documents. The information they use can then be designed into the checkwords.

CORRECTIVE POWER

Although it is rather easy to appreciate the error *de- tection* power of checkwords, their power to assist in *corrective* efforts takes many subtle forms.

CORRECTION EXAMPLE

Consider the simplified order form that might look like this (with variable information underlined):

```
+----------------------------------------------------------+
|                 O R D E R    F O R M                     |
|                                                          |
|  NUMBER 12375      SHIP TO Bill's Bargain Store          |
|                           6814 Jersey Lane               |
|                           Hunter, New York               |
|  QUANTITY PROD. NO.    DESCRIPTION                        |
|     3       12358      Baby Carriages                    |
|    64       69821      Nylon Panty Hose                  |
+------~~~~~~~~~~~~~~~~~~~~~~~~~~~~~~~~~~~~~~~~~~~~~~~~~~~----+
```

The actual message keyed from this order might be as follows (with an error in the second product number):

        12375 BBS 3 12358 BAB 64 68921 NYL

The reader should be able to see the principles on which these checkwords were extracted, and how they might be used to check the various identifiers. For example, when the erroneous code, 68921, is used to access a product record in the master inventory file, it may happen that there is no such record. In that case, the error is detected immediately.

If, however, product 68921 happens to be

        68921 SPRINKLERS, LAWN

the NYL checkword will not match either of the plausible checkwords, SPR or LAW, and a mistaken order will be prevented. Even without the original order form, there is a good chance that a human being can figure out that the digits 8 and 9 were transposed.

THE CHECKWORD LISTING

For full error detection power, the checkword should not be correlated with the identifier. The same principle holds true for error *correction*. Consider a listing of identifiers and checkwords *in sequence by checkword*. Without much design effort, we could very likely get a listing such as:

        NYL   NYLON BRIEFS   53653

        NYL   NYLON PANTY HOSE (NUTBROWN)   69821

NYL   NYLON PANTY HOSE (PEARLBEIGE)   69822

NYL   NYLON ZIPPERS   01346

If a human being uses this list to correct a product code/checkword combination of 69823 NYL, what decision would be made? It could be right, but it would have to be a guess, because the product codes are heavily correlated with product descriptions. In existing catalogs, this correlation is quite common, and must be broken by the checkword designer.

One insurance company discovered an unwanted correlation because insurance policy numbers had originally been based on the spelling of the holder's name. The designer used the checkword listing to detect the close sequential relationships between checkword and identifier. If there happens to be such a correlation in *your* design, don't panic! There is usually some natural checkword to use--even extracted from the same item in a different way.

In the NYL list, for instance, we might evaluate checkwords taken from the initial letters--but right-to-left, so as to incorporate the color information. This technique would give the following four checkwords:

BN   NYLON BRIEFS   53653

NHP   NYLON PANTY HOSE (NUTBROWN)   69821

PHP   NYLON PANTY HOSE (PEARLBEIGE)   69822

ZN   NYLON ZIPPERS   01346

Although still not perfect, this checkword dissolves much of the checkword/identifier correlation. Only in the most exceptional cases will we have to reassign catalog numbers.

OBTAINING CANDIDATE IDENTIFIERS

To correct an erroneous identifier, the human operator uses a checkword or equivalent listing stored in the operator's brain. To correct, we exchange the roles of identifier and checkword. Instead of searching the identifier index and confirming it with the checkword, we search the checkword listing and try to find a confirming identifier. If only one identifier has that checkword, it is our best candidate. If two or more are listed, we need some way to make a choice among the candidates. For instance, the checkword NHP might turn up these two:

NHP   NYLON PANTY HOSE (NUTBROWN)   69821

NHP   PLASTIC HAIR NET   45844

In automating this operation, the first problem is organizing the checkword information so a list of candidate identifiers can be efficiently retrieved. Several organizations are possible:

A table in memory (particularly in a virtual system) is the best choice if the list is sufficiently short.

Direct access to the records will usually be impossible because the file is organized by identifier, not checkword. Some data base systems, however, permit the user to pretend there is direct access by checkword.

When such direct access is not supported by the data base, an index relating checkword and identifier is required.

When an index is used, searching should be fast enough to allow the program to examine variant checkwords, in case the original checkword yields nothing, or too many candidates. Access to the records themselves need not be as fast as access to the index. Many systems won't even need to access the record to make a correction, for the index contains all needed information. In the above example, an index search for NHP would yield two candidate identifiers--69821 and 45844. The original keying was 68921, so the choice can be made solely from the similarity of the identifiers, without reference to further information that would require accessing record 69821 itself.

SELECTING THE RIGHT CANDIDATE

Human operators instantly recognize that 68921 is

very "similar" to 69821, and very "dissimilar" to
45844. When the operator is asked to make the correction, all the program need do is present the two
alternatives and await the operator's decision.

For automatic correction, we must program "similarity" tests that emulate the human operator's unconscious process. Some typical similarity tests are

EXAMPLE		*TEST*
98765	99765	*single digit substitution*
36722	37622	*adjacent pair transposition*
45839	89543	*permutation of same digits*
31255	32215	*double digit substitution*
SCREW	CREW	*truncation at beginning*
SCRAPE	SCRAP	*truncation at end*
FACULTY	FAULTY	*dropping interior symbol, or adding a symbol*

With a reasonably designed system, most corrections will be "obvious" to rather simple programmed
tests. Once in a while, there will be an ambiguous
case, such as these:

KEYED AS	*CANDIDATES*
12345	22345 *(substitute first digit)*
	12346 *(substitute fifth digit)*
12345	12354 *(adjacent transposition)*
	12344 *(single digit substitution)*
12345	43125 *(permutation)*
	11355 *(double digit substitution)*

To resolve such ambiguous cases automatically,
the program needs a ranking of the different kinds of
similarity. The highest priority is attached to the
most likely errors experienced by this system. If experience has shown that final digit substitutions are
3 times as likely as initial digit substitutions, the
choice of 12346 in the first example is 3 times more
likely to be correct than 22345. The designer will
have to decide if this margin of safety is adequate
for the system. If not, other information will have

incorporated into the decision process.

One alternative is to return control to the operator, supplying probabilities in each case, as in

UNABLE TO MAKE A RELIABLE CHOICE FOR 12345

IT HAS 75% CHANCE OF BEING 12346

AND   25% CHANCE OF BEING 22345

PLEASE ASSIST

Another alternative is to derive a *different* checkword. A search using a second checkword might disclose 3 candidates:

37869   22345   90021

For these 3, there is no ambiguity as to which is most similar to 12345.

If the second list *still* has an ambiguity, the two lists can be scanned for duplicates. Thus, if the second candidate list was

48307   22345   12845   77188

we again have an ambiguity (22345 and 12845 are almost equally similar to 12345). In this case, however, comparing the two lists resolves the ambiguity, for 22345 is the only identifier on both.

BIASED ERROR DISTRIBUTIONS

Suppose we are using a checkword with an identifier that also has a check digit--one that self-checks for all single substitution and adjacent transposition errors. If self-checking is applied before attempting to access a record, there will be 3 ways of discovering an incorrect identifier (see Figure 6.3):

a. *The self-checking number doesn't check.*

b. *The self-checking number checks, but no record is found.*

c. *The record is found, but doesn't pass the checkword test.*

In each of these 3 cases, the checkword can be

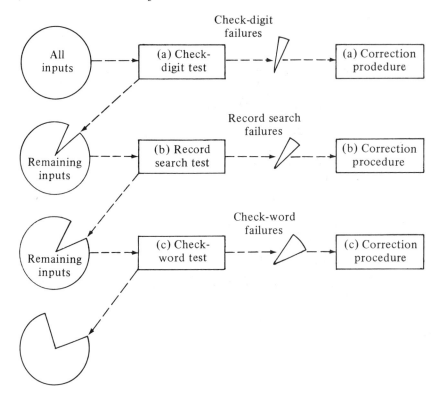

Figure 6.3   A series of correction procedures for
              inputs with different error distrib-
              utions because of prior tests.

used to attempt an automatic correction, but the correction method should be somewhat different for each.
Why? Because each successive test *filters* certain
errors out of the input reaching the next test, so the
most probable errors are different for each stage.
The three profiles are:

> *a.   The self-check fails, so a single substitution
> or adjacent transposition is quite likely to be
> the cause. Therefore, the correction procedure
> should seek candidates that are similar in these
> ways.*

> *b.   The self-check has passed, but no record has
> been found. Therefore, the corruption of the
> identifier must be more drastic than a single
> digit substitution or adjacent transposition.*

These two similarity tests are therefore excluded.

c. A record is found, but the checkword doesn't match at all. One possibility is that the check-word information is incorrect, which might be tested using alternate checkwords. The second possibility is that the identifier was picked up from some other document, so no similarity test would be meaningful. In other words, the ident-ifier isn't wrong--it's just the wrong identifier.

This combined system should correct a large maj-ority of errors, as well as recognizing most of the error situations in which automatic correction is im-possible. Other multi-level systems will have similar filtering properties. The designer's job is to char-acterize the error-distribution reaching each stage, so that sensible corrective action is applied.

WHO MAKES THE CORRECTION?

Because of their high probability of detecting and correcting identifier errors, checkword designs are particularly useful when the input is off-line. Appropriate file structures and program logic make automatic corrections in most cases, or at least pre-vent detected errors from penetrating the files.

Nevertheless, there is always a limit to automat-ic correction. In cases beyond this limit, we want the system to pass the final decision to a human oper-ator. For off-line systems, however, the "extra" in-formation in the checkword or candidate records re-duces the necessity for expensive reference to a source document. When this information is given to a human being, chances of correction are excellent.

In one library system, using the "first-three, then initial letters" system of checkwords, the search for one of Weinberg's books, *PL/I Programming Primer*, produced the checkword PLIPP (since special characters were, in this application, omitted for compatability across various terminals). When the code number was typed incorrectly, the search on checkword produced 2 candidates:

PL/I PROGRAMMING PRIMER   PLINK, PLANK, PLUNK

The operator would have little difficulty knowing which was intended for an order placed by a department of computer science and which by a kindergarten.

UNEXPECTED ERRORS

The choice between *Plink*, *Plank*, *Plunk* and *PL/I Programming Primer* could be made automatically. Information on the category of each book--perhaps the Dewey Decimal or Library of Congress code--would have to be stored, but would likely be stored for other purposes anyway. If not, an *explicit* code would have to be added to the record.

Human beings, on the other hand, can use *implicit* information, like titles, without any advance planning. The designer can foster human corrections by providing a rich variety of information. In using such implicit information, however, human beings may jump to erroneous conclusions. Some years ago, an IBM office manager secretly cancelled an order for a book entitled *The Art of Simulation*. Why? He thought it was about *acting*. The word "Primer" in the PL/I title might similarly arouse a person's thoughts of a kindergarten, but a computer wouldn't be misled by knowing too much.

Yet even a computer can know too much. Suppose the professor of computer science orders a music book for her five-year-old? Or a kindergarten teacher is studying programming at night school? If such cases are anticipated, we can provide a code indicating that corrections shouldn't be attempted--just follow the order literally.

In the end, though, there will always be a finite chance of a computer or human being jumping to the wrong conclusion. Therefore, we may be surprised by the *particular* error, but we should never be surprised that there is *some* error, even in the best of systems.

UNEXPECTED BENEFITS

Not all surprises are bad. In one national taxation center, where checkwords have been in use for over a decade, the checkword is extracted from an address. At first, there seemed to be a problem with this choice because people changed their addresses from time to time. Consequently, some perfectly valid taxpayer identifications were rejected because the address had changed.

This problem was solved when someone finally realized that it wasn't a *problem* at all, but an *opportunity*. The actual problem was the failure of taxpayers to notify the center when an address had changed. Money, bills, and receipts were mailed to incorrect addresses, but by law could not be forwarded. Returned letters generated mounds of paperwork, errors, and expense. By using the checkword failure as a *signal of a potential address change*, the taxation center converted the problem into an asset.

This example illustrates another general checkword property. We can use checkwords to check either of two things, or both together. We can verify that we have the *correct record*, or that the *record is correct*—that is, updated to match the checkword information taken from the input.

INVARIANT OR VARIANT CHECKWORDS

Perhaps the most puzzling design decision is the choice between invariant and variant checkwords—possibly because the designer is unaccustomed to allowing variation in computer systems.

INVARIANT CHECKWORDS

The only way to ensure an invariant checkword is to assign one to each identifier. Generally, each identifier has its invariant checkword "attached"—much like a check digit. The source of the checkword can be different for different identifiers, but once chosen, the checkword stays with that identifier and the identifier never gets another. Examples include:

373-467-TBLE   *a catalog number for a table*

SKY-13987-R   *catalog number for a red skyrocket*

38769/THMP	*personal identifier for someone named THOMPSON*

By using invariant checkwords, we gain several advantages:

We confirm correct identifications.

We obtain detection of 100% of single keying or handwriting errors, but not of errors involving selection of the wrong identifier, because checkword and identifier are attached.

We obtain 100% correction of single character corruption, plus a variety of other corrections.

Because we assign the checkwords, we can prevent accidental correlations that might reduce checking and correcting power.

The principal *disadvantage* of invariant checkwords is the destruction of independence needed for double checking and checking of earlier errors.

VARIANT CHECKWORDS

There is no essential reason why checkwords have to be invariant, other than the designer's fear of letting the operator derive variant ones. Checkwords work well if the same identifier may be accompanied first by one, and then by another, checkword. For example, a person could be identified by an employee number supplemented by one or more of the following checkwords:

INPUT	EXPLANATION
2345 TG	*initials, as in Tom Gilb*
2345 GIL	*leading sequence*
2345 GILT	*leading sequence, plus first initial*
2345 IVER	*street name prefix*
2345 IH2	*shorter street name prefix, with house number*
2345 1697	*last 4 phone number digits*

Advantages accruing to the user of variant check-words include the following:

Operational difficulties are lessened.

Operator comfort prevents errors.

Less training is needed.

There is less chance of destroying the system through extensions, after the original designer has departed.

More situations are covered, especially those in which checkwords cannot be applied in advance.

Errors are handled better because keying identifier and checkword are more independent.

Errors involving selection of the wrong identifier can be detected.

What do we pay for these considerable advantages? The computer may have to make more programmed searches to achieve plausible corrections. Moreover, there will be some loss of detection/correction powers, especially if we permit only one checkword per input message. In general, these disadvantages are far over-shadowed by the advantages. Programming costs and machine costs are recovered through improved operations, while error-prevention and independence make total reliability superior to invariant checkwords, even allowing for some loss of power.

HUMANIZATION POTENTIAL

Highly variant checkwords satisfy important human needs. It is neither costly, complex, difficult, nor dangerous to allow people to invent their own check-word abbreviations. Operators who don't have to know the "one single right" checkword can use whatever the source document contains.

But is this flexibility worth the risks? The source document itself will "corrupt" even the best checkword scheme with incorrect spellings, arbitrary abbreviations, and unreadable writing. So why force the operator to function on a level that clearly has no justification? Is it because the designers lack

experience with checkword systems? Do they fear complicated programming? If so, why does simpler programming justify demoralizing and dehumanizing the data
entry operators?

Besides, the programming for variant checkwords
is often trivial, especially if it doesn't have to do
a "perfect" and completely automatic job. By leaving
a few exceptionally difficult cases to human judgement,
programming costs can be slashed. Moreover, the computer logic can be designed consistently on the "safe"
side, and doubtful cases need not be approved without
human inspection.

By forcing human operators into rigid disciplines,
we are not saving design and programming work, but
merely shoving the difficulty into *other* areas. Costs
will increase, reliability will decrease, and messages
will be delayed. It's unrealistic to imagine that
people will provide accurate, unique messages that
obey all the arbitrary rules in our "Data Entry Guide."

People make mistakes. It's part of their humanity. Good designers keep this fallibility in mind.
Top designers go one step further and give people a
chance to use their adaptability as a positive factor
to overcome error--as by extracting some form of
checkword from the most astonishingly ill-prepared
document.

EVALUATING CHECKWORD DESIGNS

Consider a simple checkword scheme which employs one
identifier of the form

    67H74418F

and a checkword formed from the description of a product, such as

    PLAIN TOE SLIP ON BLACK *becomes* PTSOB

How can we estimate in advance how well such a scheme
will meet our design criteria for error detection,
location, and correction?

MATHEMATICAL ANALYSIS

As usual in statistical estimating, the mathematics will be easier if we can assume *independence* of both errors and codes. Thus, for example, if errors in identifiers are independent of errors in checkwords, and each occurs with a frequency of .01, we can assert that in only .0001 of the cases will *both* identifier and checkword be in error. Reasonable consideration must be given to operator fatigue and other factors that make for correlation of errors, so we might raise this level conservatively to .001.

If checkword and identifier are themselves independent, we should certainly be able to *correct* every single-character error. Whether we can correct the double errors depends on our rules for finding "similar" checkwords, and cannot be computed easily on a mathematical basis. Nevertheless, *detection* should be quite high--.99 of the double errors would be a conservative estimate. This would mean that no more than one in 10,000 to 100,000 entries should have undetected miskeying or miswriting errors. Inasmuch as this is far below the probable rate of errors from reading the wrong form or specifying the wrong item, further estimating in most applications would not be needed.

TESTING THE ASSUMPTIONS

On the other hand, we *may not have the independence* we desire. Looking in the same catalog, we might find

67H75418F PLAIN TOE SLIP ON BURGUNDY

which codes into

67H75418F PTSOB

which differs in only one digit from

67H74418F PTSOB

The problem arises because similar products were given similar product codes, destroying independence. Our ability to correct errors will deteriorate, as when we receive the input line:

    67H7?418F PTSOB

The best we can do here is present the operator two choices, but a source document reference will likely be needed to complete the correction.

    Even worse, we might receive

    67H<u>5</u>418F PTSOB

where the first 4 was miskeyed as a 5, making a perfectly valid, but wrong, entry. There is no way this simple system can correct this case, even with operator assistance, since there is no way it can detect anything wrong.

    Of course, a *different* system *could* make the detection, and subsequently the correction. This system might be entirely different, or it might be an "add-on" to our first design. We could use tests based on other data entered in direct connection with the product code, such as

> *Does this customer order such products?*

> *Is it reasonable, based on past experience, that he would order this many, or at this time of year?*

    With the present poorly designed product identifiers, it is unlikely that either of these tests would help much. The same customer who orders *black* slip-ons is likely to order *burgundy* ones, in approximately the same quantities, and at the same time of year.

CONSIDERING ALTERNATIVE DESIGNS

    The designer, after uncovering such flaws in a proposed system, must imagine a variety of alternatives to the design. For instance, the designer should examine *all* information entered with the product code, hoping to find something else on which to base the checkword or to supplement it. In this case, the other information might be

description	*the current candidate for check-wording, but could it be used differently?*

quantity	*likely to be the same for black and burgundy?*
price	*also likely to be the same?*
size	*the same range of choices for each color?*
ship weight	*the same for all colors?*

Another way to avoid these undetectable errors is to assign new product codes. If the codes were

67H74418F   PLAIN TOE SLIP ON BURGUNDY

93M40295J   PLAIN TOE SLIP ON BURGUNDY

a mistake in either code would be easily corrected using the checkword file index.

Assigning new codes might be out of the question because of cost involved in affecting many other areas of the business (especially a business as large as Sears, from whose catalog these examples were drawn). A partial approach would increase the identifier length with a checkword printed in the catalog--but this also has its drawbacks.

In fact, *any* approach will have drawbacks--if not, the designers wouldn't get such fabulous salaries. The designer's problem is to *evaluate* the drawbacks of alternative approaches in order to do one or more of the following things:

select one design from the others as being "superior"

uncover correctable inadequacies in one or more methods

measure the cost to be anticipated from each method, including the cost of its inadequacies

A SIMULATION APPROACH

When simple mathematical models reach their limit and the knowledge to be gained from inspection of cases has been exhausted, the designer may turn to a simulation of the best current candidate, or of alternative candidates. The easiest and most direct method of making such a simulation is to select representative input data, sprinkle it with "errors" simulating expected error patterns, and run it through the contemplated processing routines. Figure 6.4 shows the process diagram.

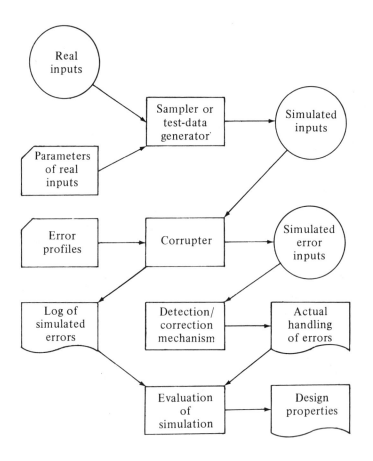

Figure 6.4 The process of simulating an input system's error detection and correction properties.

This approach was used by Weinberg and Gressett (1963) to measure the error detection properties of FORTRAN compilers. The inputs were FORTRAN programs thought to be a typical sample. The errors were based on profiles of both punching and transmission errors. Existing FORTRAN compilers were used to detect the errors.

The experiments showed that FORTRAN programs, as input to compilers, were largely self-checking against transmission errors and slightly less so against punching errors. Several weaknesses were uncovered, such as the vulnerability of programs with poorly chosen identifiers (one-character long, or with small "distances" from other identifiers). These weaknesses could be overcome by stylistic changes in program writing, but others required changes to the compilers (the detection method, in this case) to make better use of information about potential errors.

The moral from this FORTRAN simulation carries over directly into input design:

SIMULATION TESTS ASSUMPTIONS, NOT DESIGNS.

In other words, don't simulate until the design "feels good." For one thing, simulation will be more expensive than back-of-the-envelope estimates, or eyeballing the data. You want the simulation to discover whether your pencil slipped or your eye blinked.

Another way to think about simulation is this:

DON'T SHOW OFF THE DESIGN, SHOW IT UP.

Don't try to show that your good feeling was right. Try to show it was *wrong*. Then, if you try very hard, and honestly, and still fail to show up the design, or collapse your assumptions, you can be confident that someone else *won't* show it up--or collapse the system itself.

OFF-LINE SIMULATION

How could we use simulation to evaluate the major contending alternatives to the "plain toe slip on"

checkword system? The first step is to create a file
of simulated transactions. This file might be extracted from existing input files, or generated by a test
data generator--perhaps supplemented by some hand-made
cases.

The next step is to introduce errors into the
simulated input file, according to some contemplated
profile. Error *rates* are inflated so that each input
has one or more errors. If possible, identifying information is placed with the transaction (to be ignored by the input program) specifying just what error
was inserted. If this information cannot be placed
within the input (as with FORTRAN comments), a *parallel listing* is made to assist in evaluating the simulation results.

The third step is to pass these erroneous records
against the input routines--or a hand simulation of
them. The actual error handling can be matched with
the original record and error information to produce
both quantitative and qualitative information. For
example, how many errors were

> *detected and corrected automatically*
>
> *detected, but correctable only with operator
> intervention*
>
> *detected, but correctable only by an operator
> having a source document*
>
> *detected, but uncorrectable even with the aid of
> a source document*
>
> *undetected*
>
> *detected, but "corrected" to the wrong values*

If our sampling is adequate, the counts will give
us good design figures, when scaled to actual error
rates. We repeat the exercise for promising alternative designs until we find the desired level of per-
formance--and *confidence* in that performance.

"LIVE" SIMULATION

In the end, the *implementation* of any system is a

simulation, too, especially if properly *instrumented* to tell how it's performing. It simulates the *future* behavior of *itself*. Although it may seem to be a *free* simulation, it will be expensive if the design assumptions turn out poorly. Yet, it need not always be this way, especially in checkword and other "natural" input systems.

Suppose that our checkword system is being contemplated as a *replacement* for an existing input system. If we are extracting the checkword from existing material, there is no need for operators to change their keying pattern under the new system. We implement the checkword logic, but make its application *optional*, depending on which port and/or operator is providing the input.

Under such a system, selected operators use the checkword system while the others continue to use the former system. A similar approach is taken if the checkword requires *additional* information, but its *use* can be made optional. Some operator training will be required, but the principle is the same in the two situations.

By reducing the number of operators on the live system, we limit our risk. If the checkwords turn out to produce the desired properties, the remaining operators are cut over one at a time.

WHY WAIT?

If the live simulation tests go poorly, we can cut back immediately to the old system. Alternatively, we can redesign the system one step at a time, and test each new part in exactly the same way. If we have done our design well, the new system--even with its flaws--will probably be better than the old one. In that case, we simply make the new one into the old one--so we don't lose *all* benefits because of a few small problems.

For example, we might find that our present design is quite vulnerable to "color" errors, as between BLACK and BURGUNDY. To "correct" this problem, we might have to wait for the next catalog, yet color errors might be

fewer than .01% of all transactions

*not too costly, in general, because many cust-
omers will simply accept a substitute color*

handled even worse in the old system

Under these circumstances, we would go live with the
flawed system--possibly forever, possibly until the
catalog numbers are changed, or possibly until we can
incorporate supplementary information into the checkword. In the meantime, we can give an extra pair of
panty hose to customers inconvenienced by a color
error. There's no sense making other people bear the
brunt of our inadequate input system.

A SUMMARY OF EXPECTED ATTRIBUTES

The following is a simplified multidimensional view of
the normal attributes which the designer can expect
when specifying checkwords. The designer must calculate or otherwise estimate the more accurate attributes
for his particular implementation in order to compare
this option against other design alternatives.

PRODUCTIVITY

Checkword methods, correctly applied, can be expected to raise overall productivity, even when the
major focus is on raising reliability. Like any redundancy technique, however, the *first impression* may
be that checkwords will reduce productivity--at least
in the sense of raw counts of keying effort. Therefore, the designer must give full consideration to
error detection/location/correction/prevention as part
of the cost of productivity, and not be swayed by early, simplistic arguments about "productivity."

In cases designed by or with the authors, the introduction of a checkword (as a major factor, usually
combined with other appropriate techniques) gave immediate productivity increases for the data entry
staff alone. In addition, other clerical work such as

correcting and checking were substantially reduced.
In several cases, more than doubling of productivity
resulted, and once a factor of 8 was achieved by

eliminating overtime

reassigning clerical staff

*increasing the output while these reductions
took place*

A major factor in the increased output was the more
human, responsible task given the operators, and
greater pride in a system that obviously *cared* about
reliability.

RELIABILITY

We have seen how checkwords can be designed to
provide arbitrarily high reliability--up to the point
where the "blunder rate" makes more reliability fruitless. Checkword systems are easily designed to detect
and correct 99.99% of single character errors, and
will have high probabilities of detecting and correcting other errors. A proper computation of the probabilities rests both on the particular design and on the
degree of independence of checkword and identifier
errors. Properly designed checkword systems are not
limited to detecting and correcting keying errors, but
can reach errors occuring at or close to the data
source.

PORTABILITY

As long as hardware is not being downgraded,
which is certainly a rare event in computing, it is
possible to design checkwords that are arbitrarily
portable. Since they will be more reliable, checkwords will contribute to the overall portability of
the system.

IMPLEMENTATION EASE

Programming difficulty can range from simple
comparisons to elaborate "spelling correction" routines

affecting the entire file organization. Programming
can be done incrementally, so we need not incur one
huge implementation crisis.

HARDWARE RESOURCES

Extra keying could conceivably lead to an increase in the number of key stations, compensated by less
correction effort elsewhere. Alternatively, operators
may become more efficient overall, depending on the
existing system. Some program space and time will be
needed, but the biggest additional hardware burden is
likely to be in secondary storage space--and time, if
multiprogramming is not used. Through the use of existing information in records as well as indices,
rather than full file accesses, these requirements can
be kept within specified bounds. A tradeoff of space
for processing time can be made by keeping an additional field or fields for a checkword, to avoid time-
consuming scanning to extract checkwords from text.

Detection logic can be as small as a single machine instruction. The infrequently invoked automatic
correction (of both checkwords and identifiers) will
require

> *extra program, which may safely reside in virtual
> or segmented storage*

> *slight extra CPU time, which will generally not
> be noticed in the overall run time*

> *possible extra indices to the files or data base,
> either in main storage or on secondary storage,
> or both.*

SECURITY

Checkwords may be used in the same way as a security oriented secret password, as long as the method
of deriving checkwords is not known to outsiders. As
with repeated codes, checkwords are easier to *read*,
but more difficult to *alter*. Because the information
making up the checkword is not derived from the original code itself (as in repeated codes) anyone trying

to alter a checkword (or access a record through a checkworded identifier) is going to have a hard time succeeding. Instrumentation for normal checkword use can identify various forms of attempted intrusion.

EXTENDABILITY

Checkword systems are inherently extendable, because of their naturalness. When adding subsequent checkword/identifier pairs, however, new algorithms may prove confusing to the operators. Automatic extraction circumvents this problem, as will making the two algorithms simple variants of one another--making the operator's job *easier* as the system is extended.

Because checkword effectiveness depends on the probability of coincidences, large increases in the underlying identifier set could decrease performance. Performance will be severely degraded if new identifiers are added in such a way as to make them highly correlated with their checkwords.

DESIGN EXERCISES

1. Rexamine the first exercise of Chapter V (page 151) to see if further improvement in the design can be achieved through the use of checkwords for some input elements. Discuss how checkwords affect the performance of the design, or if not, why not.

2. Explain why properly designed check digits prevent any two identifiers from being only one digit different. Suggest other design schemes that have this property, especially ones that can be used with identifiers containing non-numeric characters. Discuss how these schemes will behave with respect to automatic correction in conjunction with checkwords.

3. Describe how a distributor might assign product codes without clustering. In particular, be sure your design prevents the assignment system from breaking down after the initial assignment is made under supervision of the designer--as day-to-day additions are

made to the product list. How can a checkword scheme monitor this assignment to ensure that it doesn't deteriorate?

4. Using an identifier/description file available to you, simulate the performance of at least two checkword designs. Discuss how your conclusions might be affected by sampling errors, and what could be done to avoid them. Discuss how the two designs are affected as the file grows 10%, 100%, 1000%.

5. Would birthdates make reasonable checkwords for a name identifier? How many reasons can you imagine for this kind of checkword system breaking down? Suggest a design to make the birthdate checkword function well in a factory work reporting system.

6. Would telephone numbers make good checkwords for medical doctor names, in patient expense reporting for insurance? What if these numbers were preprinted on the doctor's stationery? What happens if mother and daughter were sharing the same office? What could be done about it?

7. Use the telephone directory to simulate manually a checkword system to correct spelling of names, using telephone numbers as checkwords. Try slightly misspelled names with perfect or corrupted checkwords. How does the length of the checkword affect performance in detection and correction?

8. Explain the use of a checkword in a program library to prevent accidental update to the wrong module or version of a module. Explain why a scrambled checkword, provided by the system after each update, is superior to a simple version number.

Chapter VII

Adaptive Checking

The Butcher would gladly have talked till next day,
    But he felt that the Lesson must end,
And he wept with delight in attempting to say
    He considered the Beaver his friend.

While the Beaver confessed, with affectionate looks
    More eloquent even than tears,
It had learnt in ten minutes far more than all books
    Would have taught it in seventy years.

                    --*The Hunting of the Snark, Fit the Fifth*

Conventional message design methods tend to underutil-
ize available technology. Checkword techniques are
frequently ignored because the designer doesn't realize the potential of on-line storage. Or, he may be
stopped by the lack of a clear idea about how on-line
storage can assist data entry. He may fear a seventy-
year start-up effort and even heavier maintenance
costs.

    In this chapter, we will see how a system can
learn more "in ten minutes" than we could provide by

non-adaptive methods in seventy years. Moreover, the
adaptive system and the operator will enjoy a relationship of mutual cooperation--each will consider the
other a friend.

LIMIT CHECKING

Any introductory systems design text is likely to mention the concept of checking quantitative data for
reasonable values using a limit test:

IF QUANTITY-ORDERED IS GREATER THAN 10000

OR LESS   THAN   1

THEN PERFORM ERROR-ROUTINE.

Real data processing environments do use limit checking, but mostly as a defense against the grossest
errors. Numerous cases that human beings would recognize as erroneous are allowed to pass the limit check.
If only there were some way of making the computer
learn the way people do, limit checking could achieve
the promise made in so many introductory texts.

LIMITS TO LIMIT CHECKING

What factors limit the usefulness of limit checking? The first factor is the *variability* found in any
large data base. One exceptional circumstance forces
us to expand the limit for all other amounts in the
same category. The only way to narrow the limits is
to reduce the number of items in each category and
provide separate limits for each.

The next factor is the *cost* of determining and
recording the *large number of limits* we need to achieve "tight" reasonableness checks. Even if we could
stand this initial cost, limits *change over time* for
such reasons as seasonal variations, working holidays,
economic conditions, market growth or decline, new
laws and regulations, and sales campaigns. If the
limits are to remain useful, they must reflect these
variations, but the more closely they do, the more
their maintenance costs.

NEW TECHNOLOGICAL OPPORTUNITIES

A few years ago, storage limitations would have prevented our placing separate limits on a large number of quantities. Now, storage is plentiful and relatively cheap.

Until recently, stored information was clumsy and expensive to access for frequent updating. Now, cooperation between people and machines is convenient and cheap, through interactive data entry.

In the recent past, computer logic was expensive, so we couldn't afford to put much logic near the actual data source. At the same time, data transmission was unreliable, costly, and slow, so we couldn't afford to connect the source to a central computer, either. Now, we have many cost-effective ways of providing close cooperation between a computer and the people at the data source--people who can give accurate and timely information on what is reasonable and what is not.

PROPERTIES OF EFFECTIVE LIMIT CHECKING

These new technological opportunities can be combined into a limit checking system that overcomes the previous limitations. The system would have the following properties:

It will keep a large number and variety of limits to ensure "tight" checking, no matter how big the system ultimately grows.

It will use its experience and the judgement of its operators to adjust each limit automatically as required by changes over time.

No special initial cost will be required, for the system can start from conservative initial limits and adjust them automatically as it operates.

The system will not attempt "complete" checking. Instead it will strive for a well-balanced cooperation between operator and machine, in order to achieve error prevention in proportion to error seriousness.

In effect, the limit checking system will be counted a success if nobody notices it--that it neither does too much nor doesn't do enough.

We can appreciate the adaptive limit checking system by following a sample dialogue:

INTERACTION	*REMARKS*
2345 BLT	*Order entry, with checkword: a request for product 2345.*
<u>PLEASE GIVE QUANTITY</u>	*Item code is confirmed, but no quantity was given. Program is forgiving and courteous.*
24	*Program also accepts such forms as +24, 24.0, or 0024. It is variation tolerant, to a reasonable degree.*
	Limit here is currently 33, so order can be accepted without comment. The limit is updated as needed in the product record for product 2345. No update is needed on this transaction.
. . .	
35 2345 BLT	*At some later time, 35 items are ordered.*
<u>35 1/2" BOLTS</u> <u>ACCEPTED AS ORDER.</u> <u>PLEASE NOTE THAT IT</u> <u>IS SLIGHTLY ABOVE</u> <u>PREVIOUS EXPERIENCE</u> <u>LEVEL OF 33.</u>	*Because the limit of 33 has been exceeded, some sort of warning will be given, but since the system has a tol- erance of 10%, it is only a warning. Completeness of warning will be adjusted to terminal hardware speed.*

The user has an opportunity to revoke this order, but the default action is merely to proceed to the next

order entry. In the meantime, the computer has *adjust-*
ed the limit to 35, as this seems to be an acceptable
maximum for this product.

INTERACTION	REMARKS
INTERACTION	*REMARKS*
40 2345 BLT	*Product number checks, and format is right, but this time the quantity is a bit too far above warning level.*
QUANTITY OF 40 IS SLIGHTLY HIGH BASED ON PREVIOUS EXPERI-ENCE. MORE REASON-ABLE HIGH WOULD BE 35 FOR 1/2" BOLT 2345 IF 40 IS CORRECT, PLEASE CONFIRM	*Notice the output message design. It is not a gener-alized WRONG QUANTITY mess-age, but makes use of the variables involved to make it quite clear to the oper-ator which factors are in-volved in the decision.*
40	*This is a confirmation by the operator, who could also correct either a quan-tity error or identifier error--or perhaps seek more information.*
40 1/2" BOLT 2345 PLACED ON ORDER	*The system needn't bother the operator with the fact that the limit may now have been adjusted to 40.*
. . .	
38 2345 BLT	*Since the upper limit is now 40, this new transact-ion is accepted without comment.*
. . .	
50 2345 BLT 50	*In this case, the operator recognizes in advance that 50 is an exceptional order-- perhaps there has been a special authorization on the source document--and avoids a possible time-con-suming interaction by*

INTERACTION	REMARKS
	repeating the quantity. This form can be used to prevent adjustment of the limits, since the order is recognized as exceptional.
<u>FIFTY 1/2" BOLT 2345</u> <u>50 PLACED ON ORDER</u>	*Just in case, though, the order is confirmed, requiring no interaction by operator if it is correct.*

When cases are recognizably exceptional, it may be good design to feed back a transformed version in the confirmation. In this case, numbers are transcribed into words and a fuller product description is given. It's not really needed here, but look at the next case:

INTERACTION	REMARKS
50,00 2345 BLT	*Comma was punched instead of period, but this program simply ignores commas, as in 10,000,000.*
<u>FIVE THOUSAND BOLTS</u> <u>2345 IS MUCH LARGER</u> <u>THAN EARLIER EXPERI-</u> <u>ENCE. IF CONFIRMED</u> <u>SALES DIRECTOR WILL</u> <u>BE ALERTED.</u>	*Note reaction to threatened security of inventory by theft or embezzlement. Operator need not be informed that auditors will be alerted in any case, to prevent too much probing of the system's limits.*
50 2345 BLT	*This is all that should be needed for correction, if limit is now 50.*
<u>FIFTY 1/2" BOLT 2345</u> <u>50 PLACED ON ORDER</u>	*Confirmation of correction.*

AUTOMATIC ADJUSTMENTS

In the preceeding rather simplified example, raising the limits depends on

orders actually experienced

human judgement as to which orders are typical and which are exceptional

Because there is no provision for *lowering* the limits, the limit will be "the largest regular order ever experienced for this item." Without supplementary adjustments, this limit would grow ever wider, and limit checking would grow less effective.

LIMITING THE LIMITS

Because we had an order for 10,000 American flags in July 1976 doesn't mean we'll get a similar order in March 1982. We might have to wait until July 2076 to see such a huge flag order again. To keep the limits under control, there must be some way of *forgetting* some of the past.

On the other hand, an order of 50 air-conditioners in July 1976 probably suggests that a similar order in August would be reasonable. Consequently, there must be some way of *remembering* the past, too.

What the system must do is *strike a balance* between remembering and forgetting. One effective technique is to forget a certain fraction of the limit each month (or week, quarter, or whatever cycle seems appropriate to the situation). If the limit on air-conditioners in July was 50, a 30% monthly reduction would produce a reasonable limit of 35 for August. If no larger orders were received by the time December brought us Winter's cold, the limit would be down to a very sensible 8 air-conditioners.

RECOVERY FROM POOR DECISIONS

Many designers get cold chills thinking about leaving decisions to the computer or its operator (or, in fact, to anyone but designers). If asked to justify their fears, they will produce examples such as this dialogue:

INTERACTION	*REMARKS*
353 2345 BLT 353	*Operator indicates an exceptionally large order.*

INTERACTION	REMARKS
<u>THREE HUNDRED FIFTY-</u> <u>THREE 1/2" BOLT 2345</u> <u>IS VERY MUCH LARGER</u> <u>THAN PREVIOUS EXPERI-</u> <u>ENCE. PLEASE CONFIRM.</u>	*But this is too large for the system to accept un-challenged.*
353	*Operator really has this order.*
<u>THREE HUNDRED FIFTY-</u> <u>THREE 1/2" BOLT 2345</u> <u>353 PLACED ON ORDER</u> <u>WILL 353 BE A BETTER</u> <u>LIMIT IN FUTURE?(Y/N)</u>	*System has little choice but to accept and log on an exception report. But adjusting the limit is another matter.*
YES	*System accepts various forms of Y, and now sets the limit to 353.*

This operator happened to exercise poor judgement, for the largest order in the entire succeeding year is 100. The decision was misplaced in the operator's hands. The system should put such a large limit change in the hands of a responsible executive. But executives can be wrong, too. Passing *too many* such decisions to executives or designers would defeat the purpose of self-adjustment. Besides, if there is an automatic downward adjustment of limits by even 10% per month, we can't be hurt too badly on this one product.

In the first month, the amount of 353 is adjusted to 318. In succeeding months it becomes 286, 257, 231, 208, 187, 168, 151, 136, 122, 110, and 99--so that after 12 months it has succeeded in restoring itself approximately to the largest order experienced. If the business is very volatile, it will be best to have a faster damper effect. A 20% reduction per month drops a doubled limit to its old value in just 3 months, as when 100 doubles to 200 and then drops to 160, 128, and 82, in successive months.

INTERACTION LEVEL

In a limit checking system, the amount of various

types of interaction can be set by the system designer by changing

the method of raising limits

the method of narrowing limits

the parameters of limit adjustment

the relationship among limits for various operator/machine interactions

We can recognize many levels of interaction in such a system. For each interaction, the designer can set down a rate of occurrence he feels will meet the specifications, as in the following list:

LEVEL OF INTERACTION	*DESIRED % OF ORDERS*
1. Accept automatically........	99.000
2. Accept with warning, adjust the limit......................	.800
3. Accept with confirmation, but do not adjust..............	.100
4. Accept with confirmation, and adjustment also confirmed...	.050
5. Put on warning report if adjustment confirmed...........	.020
6. Put on warning report if order confirmed................	.015
7. Put on warning report even if order is not confirmed.......	.010
8. Adjustment not confirmable by operator acting alone........	.004
9. Order not confirmable by operator acting alone..........	.001

In other words, in this system, 1 out of 100,000 orders will require management confirmation to be accepted, and 5 out of 10,000 will appear on a management report as some sort of exception. For the most part, such a system operates like a set of "rings of defense"-- with the inner rings penetrated least frequently.

MONITORING PERFORMANCE

For reporting purposes, the "rings of defense" may overlap--as when we take a random *sample* of situations not otherwise seen by management. Such a sample might provide a few instances of each level, such as level 2, "accept with warning, adjust the limit." If one of the limits was being gradually "nursed" up, either by market forces or by some fraudulent scheme, management might not see it reported at all unless sampling is done.

In any system that adjusts its own behavior, we have the opportunity to monitor all sorts of interesting information--information which should, perhaps, be monitored in less dynamic systems but which seldom is. For instance, we might monitor

a. *samples of transactions, as explained above*

b. *all items whose limits go above some absolute quantity*

c. *all items whose limits go above some absolute money limit, such as 100 x $5 or 1,000 x 50¢.*

d. *items showing rapid rise or decline in limits*

e. *items showing high rates of interaction*

f. *items showing unusual types of interaction*

g. *overall statistics on types of interaction.*

Using statistics as in (g), the designer can see whether performance criteria set down in the design are being met. If not, he can search for the source of the deviation, and either change the source or adjust the levels of acceptance or the method of computing limits. If, for instance, too many transactions were giving level 2 warnings, and not enough were being accepted automatically, he can adjust the tolerance slightly upwards.

In short, even though the system is "self" adjusting, the designer will have to provide for monitoring its self-adjusting behavior. In that way, people remain in charge, while computers do the work.

OTHER KINDS OF LIMIT ADJUSTMENT

A system of fixed periodic adjustments is simple to un-
derstand--an important attribute of any dynamically
self-adjusting system. Before embarking on more complex schemes of limit adjustment, the designer should
be sure--perhaps by a small simulation or actual test
trials--that the simpler scheme won't do the job as
well. But, if fixed periodic percentages don't work
well, there are a variety of other available adjustments.

MEAN VALUE

One approach is based on keeping a true *mean value*
of orders and then setting interaction limits based on
variations around (or simply above) the mean. To keep
a mean value for an item, there must be two values
saved--the total number of values going into the mean
(n), and the total value accumulated (t). The mean
may be computed anew by dividing t by n at any time,
and the two values must be updated with every trans-
action--which may be a disadvantage of this method,
if we have no other use for this information.

STANDARD DEVIATION

A simple multiple of the mean value can be used
for each limit. Checks based on mean values can work
well in applications where the quantity being checked
is "normally" distributed around the mean. Such normal distributions are found in places like these:

> *settings of monitoring devices in automatic
> control systems*
>
> *test scores or opinion surveys*
>
> *stock or commodity prices*

Naus (1975) surveys methods for deciding what
values are "extreme" when distributions are normal.
Most techniques require a second parameter descriptive
of the normal distribution--the *standard deviation*.

To compute the standard deviation in addition to the mean, one more value must be retained (see Cotton, 1975).

If the distribution is normal, we can easily set interaction levels on the basis of mathematical theory.

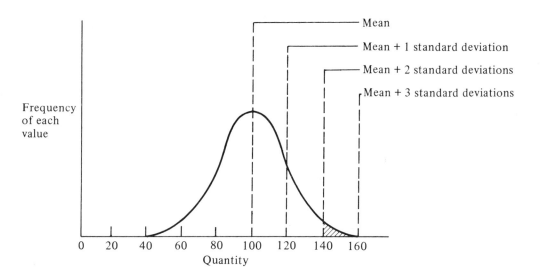

Figure 7.1   Normal curve of quantities with mean of 100 and standard deviation of 20.

Figure 7.1 shows a typical normal distribution, with a mean of 100 and a standard deviation of 20.   The shaded area represents those values that are above the mean plus two standard deviations (100 + 2x20 = 140). Statistical theory says that out of 100,000 values from this distribution, 2100 will be above 140.   Therefore, setting 140 as a limit check will produce some kind of check for 2.1% of the cases.

Placing the limit at 160 (mean plus 3 standard deviations) would reduce the interactions to about 100 in 100,000, or .1%.   To get an interaction level between these two, we consult tables of the normal distribution found in any statistics textbook.

One further advantage of the standard deviation for limit checking is its symmetry in the normal distribution.   Where abnormally *low* values are also to be checked, the same tables can be used to set interaction levels. Thus, for instance, in the distribution of Figure 7.1, .1% of transactions should be below 40--the mean *minus* 3 standard deviations.

OTHER DISTRIBUTIONS

When the input values follow normal distributions, the designer can draw upon powerful mathematical models to predict system performance with great accuracy. Few quantities in the business world, however, follow a normal distribution. For instance, order quantities tend to be very *skewed*, or very *clustered* around certain typical values. In such cases, the mean and standard deviation alone will not give us useful limit checking behavior.

In some cases, we can find other simple mathematical distributions that model our input distributions.

Size of order	1	2	3	4	5	6	7	over 7
Observed	101	145	99	42	7	4	2	0
Expected from Poisson distribution	107	141	93	41	14	4	1	0

Figure 7.2   A Poisson distribution (scaled to 1 instead of 0) compared with an observed quantity pattern.

Figure 7.2 shows a sampling of 400 order quantities for lamps from a lighting distributor. Pairs of lamps are more frequent (145) than single lamps (101), but larger orders are also experienced. The mean order quantity is 2.43 lamps, from which a Poisson distribution can be computed giving the values shown in the last line of the Figure. (The Poisson distribution here is for mean 1.43, then scaled up to 2.43, because orders of zero are never experienced, although the first Poisson value is zero.)

In this instance, the distribution models ordering behavior remarkably well. For instance, the Poisson distribution predicts that with 6 as the limit
check value, 1.25% of orders will trigger a limit
check. In the actual sample, 1.5% of the orders are
above that value.

The advantage of fitting a distribution to the
experienced values is that only a few parameters need
to be saved. In the Poisson, for instance, only the
mean value is needed. Such distributions can be stud-
ied in a variety of textbooks, such as Parzen (1960).
If we can't find a good fit, though, we can always use
a *table* instead of a statistical function--at the cost
of some storage.

STATIC ADJUSTMENTS

At times, a more-or-less *static* adjustment to a
self-adjusting system may prove useful. If the business is seasonable, limits on orders may be stretched
in the high season and contracted in the low, by fixed
amounts. If certain customers are known to order in
larger quantities, we may make a "customer class" adjustment to the limit. Similarly, if one of these
large customers makes a big order, we may discount the
order by the customer class adjustment before using it
to reset the limit.

To illustrate, suppose that class A customers are
allowed to order 3 times the ordinary limit without
triggering any interaction. Then if the limit on a
product is 120, and an A customer orders 300, the 300
will be divided by 3 for purposes of comparison with
the limit of 120. Since 300/3 = 100 is less than 120,
neither warning nor limit adjustment would be made.
We could make the customer classification self-adjusting, too, based on a history of previous orders.

PATTERN CHECKING

A limit check by its very nature is likely to catch
many of the embarrassingly *large* orders, which is why
limit checks have been so popular, even in their crude

form, in data processing. Less frequently seen is another type of checking humans can do--spotting deviations from a pattern. Watch the human clerk when someone orders a quantity that breaks the established
patterns--like an order for 7 eggs or one stocking.

Many items are habitually ordered in dozens,
others in pairs, units, fours, tens, twenties, hundreds, or gross. Some items will have two or three
characteristic patterns--they might be ordered in 12,
24, or 144, but seldom in other quantities. Or the
pattern might be 1, 10, 20, 30, 40, 50, 60, 70, 80,
90, 100--something the limit check will not help, except at the upper end.

FIXED PATTERNS

Suppose we assume that each product has but *one*
pattern of order quantity, with a small number of deviations. One way of improving validity checking is to
record this pattern within the records for which it
applies. We might, for instance, set aside a single-
character field like this:

VALUE	MEANING *(in terms of normal pattern)*
D	*DOZENS are the normal pattern (12, 24, ..)*
T	*TENS are the norm (10, 20, 30, ...)*
E	*EVENS (2, 4, 6, ...)*
5	*FIVES (5, 10, 15, ...)*
P	*PACKAGE (that is, examine the number-in-a-package field, given in the same record, to find a value for which even multiples are ordered)*
A	*ANY (only the limit check applies)*

The quantity control logic will (in addition to
the limit check) test the quantity against the set of
rules which apply for that record. Warnings will be
issued unless the pattern matches. Initial setting of
the pattern character can be based on product characteristics or computer analysis of actual order patterns
experienced.

CHANGING THE PATTERN

The system can help in manual adjustment or in its own self-adjustment by creating additional fields to record such information as

number of approved quantities not matching the pattern

number of errors caught by the pattern check

total number of quantities received by the system

This information tells whether or not the pattern is useful as a check. It does not, however, indicate what *other* pattern might be better. To do that, we would have to record more detail about the pattern of inputs over time.

THE BIT STRING APPROACH

Information about the *entire* history of different input quantities can be kept in various ways. A rather general approach can be implemented using a bit string with one position to represent each different quantity, as in Figure 7.3. If the programming language or other factors prohibit bit strings, a similar scheme can be constructed using one character per possible quantity--with concomitant increase in storage requirements.

Bit position	1	2	3	4	5	6	7	8	9	10	11	12	13	14	15
Bit value	0	1	0	1	1	0	0	0	0	1	0	0	0	0	0

Figure 7.3 A bit string representing the order quantities 2, 4, 5, and 10 as the typical pattern.

Assuming that 99% or more of our orders are for 100 items or less, this scheme would require a string length of 100, because we are only trying to warn about quantities within the limit. Actually, *two* such strings will be required, which we could conveniently name

LAST-MONTH-HAD-THIS

THIS-MONTH-HAD-THIS

In each bit position, the system marks quantities that occur by making them 1, so that a pattern starting with 11000100000100000 in LAST-MONTH-HAD-THIS would say that we had *previously experienced* quantities of 1, 2, 6, and 12.

An interaction with the system might look something like this, starting with a product that has never been ordered in this particular quantity-- perhaps a new product:

INTERACTION	*REMARKS*
4 5678 CSTR	*The bits in the fourth position of the two strings are zero, so the interaction is invoked.*
FOUR IS UNUSUAL QUANTITY FOR HEAVY DUTY CASTER NUMBER 5678 ARE YOU SURE IT'S CORRECT?	*The friendly warning, given because of new product.*
CORRECT	*We can accept various kinds of agreement or confirmation in our system. The 4th bit of THIS-MONTH-HAD-THIS is now set to 1.*
(time passes)	
4 5678 CSTR	*The 4th bit is tested and found to be 1, so the quantity of 4 is passed without comment.*
(a month passes)	*THIS-MONTH-HAD-THIS is moved into LAST-MONTH-HAD-THIS and THIS-MONTH-HAD-THIS is set to all zeros.*

INTERACTION	*REMARKS*
4 5678 CSTR	*The 4th bit of LAST-MONTH-HAD-THIS is found to be 1, so the quantity of 4 is passed without comment. The 4th bit of THIS-MONTH-HAD-THIS is set to 1 to record that a 4 was recently experienced.*

In this manner, the system can "remember" which quantities it has seen for which products for between one and two months.

VARIATIONS

A variant of the bit string system could make the recall interval any desired length. Another change would base the remembering on the *frequency* of experiencing each value. These variants would exchange more secondary storage for greater precision in the adaptation.

In some applications, we could adopt an approach to save secondary storage without sacrificing precision. Instead of one bit for each *value*, the system uses one bit for each *pattern*--as illustrated in Figure 7.4.

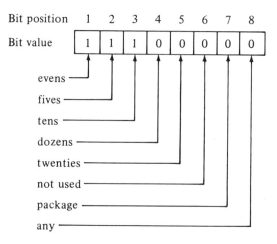

Figure 7.4   A variant scheme for storing common patterns.

The illustrated item has experienced orders in even numbers (bit 1), fives (bit 2), and tens (bit 3), but never in dozens or twenties. One bit here is reserved for expansion to new patterns at some future date, one is for items that have a standard package, and one is to indicate that all patterns are permitted for a particular item.

With this set of patterns, a quantity of 4 would update only "evens." A quantity of 20 would update evens, fives, tens, and twenties.

The imaginative designer will be able to create other variants of the pattern checking approach. To stimulate the imagination, there is a growing literature on *pattern recognition* (see, for example, Young and Calvert, 1974, or Tou and Gonzalez, 1974) and *artificial intelligence* (see, for example, Hunt, 1975; Nilsson, 1971; Slagle, 1971; or Jackson, 1974). Some of the research systems are beginning to bear fruit in practical applications.

CHARACTERISTICS

A designer need not, however, rely on sophisticated schemes to achieve adaptive pattern checking. The simple schemes sketched above demonstrate all the essential elements of the adaptive pattern checking approach:

recording experienced patterns for each item

remembering those patterns, but not forever

setting up an interaction when a quantity is encountered that is not remembered from the recent past

Some environments will be much more patterned than others, so it will be difficult to guarantee a particular frequency with which warnings will be given. As the system operates, however, it will provide information about the behavior of the environment. This information will give better control on the interaction frequency, but will also impact diverse areas of the business--such as, establishing new warehouse procedures, issuing sales bonuses, or creating new approaches to packaging our products.

By adjusting the updating cycle, we can adjust the length of time the previous experience is kept in memory. Longer memory will mean a smaller rate of interaction. If we eliminate forgetting altogether, we get a system that will accept any order quantity that had *ever* been experienced since the creation of the system. Interaction may be low, but poor checking may be the price paid for that low interaction.

The bit string system has the advantage that it can be *started up* adaptively, with minimal excess interaction, merely by making all the initial LAST-MONTH-HAD-THIS strings equal to all 1 bits. There will be no warnings at all in the first month of operation. Experience from the month will accumulate in THIS-MONTH-HAD-THIS. When the master file is saved on the monthly backup, and THIS-MONTH-HAD-THIS is moved to LAST-MONTH-HAD-THIS, the system starts giving warnings for any quantity that had not been experienced in the previous month--giving a nice smooth and cheap inauguration.

NON-NUMERIC PATTERNS

There's nothing in the bit string approach that says the positions of the string have to represent *quantities*. *Any patterned property* can be represented in this way, and the same adaptive scheme applied. Because the variant schemes are equivalent to the bit string approach in logic, any one of them can be applied to non-quantity patterns.

To take just one example, an engineering/programming firm uses a labor distribution program to allocate charges to about 200 contracts pending at any one time. Input comes from technical people who fill out cards attributing each portion of their labor to specific projects. Using a bit string approach, they are able to detect when a person makes the first charge to a particular contract. The input operator is then prompted to enter an authorization code, or to confirm the correctness of the charge.

A similar approach has been used to detect when a

customer orders a specific class of product for the first time. In fact, the approach can be used in any situation where input behavior is stable for long periods, with breaks in the pattern suggesting possible error-prone entries.

ADAPTIVE INITIALIZATION

Adaptive systems are particularly useful in spotting situations where a long-established pattern breaks. How, then, are they put in operation to begin with, when there is no past history on which to base a pattern? Surprisingly, as we have seen, most adaptive systems have a "natural" startup, as in

> *limit checking, which can be started by checking any value until limits are established, or by a single plausible value, which rapidly adjusts to something reasonable*

> *pattern checking, which can be started by setting every case to "seen last month" and allowing patterns to become established*

In fact, one of the beauties of adaptive checking is the property of *equifinality* (Weinberg, 1975), which says that it isn't really critical *where* you start the system, for it will sooner or later come to the desired state by its own actions. The property of equifinality is so useful, and so different from the usual experience of designers with non-adaptive systems, that it will be worthwhile to consider building it into systems not otherwise adaptive.

EXAMPLE: ACCOUNT STATUS QUERIES

Consider the case of a savings bank which made direct use of the equifinality principle to adjust its account data to the use of account-holder birthdate as a security password. The bank wanted to provide telephone inquiry service, but for six months had troubled over the difficulty and expense of "getting all the birthdates before we can start." This was the wrong problem formulation, and the problem was solved only after giving up on such an all-or-none approach in favor of a gradual one.

In the new design, each *inquiring* account holder was asked to give his date of birth. If this agreed with a previously registered date, the account balance information was released.

If the date had not yet been registered, some other criterion (such as telephone number) was used to check. When the operator was satisfied, the birth date was inserted in the record for the next time an inquiry was made. Eventually, all customers (that is, all who ever cared to make phone inquiries) were converted to the birthdate check, without any "extra" effort, and no measurable cost other than a little programming and operator training.

EXAMPLE: A LIBRARY DATA BASE

A similar approach can be made to upgrading the information in any existing files that are interrogated on-line. A library, to take another example, made the mistake of converting to an on-line checkout system using only call number (book code) information. Full title and author information was not entered into the data base because of the enormity of the job. Therefore, only a code such as QA397.22H was entered for each book.

Actually, it wasn't a mistake in the sense that they could not have afforded to key author and title information for all existing books, and in the sense that all their future books would get author and title as a byproduct of a cataloging service they started at the same time. But user complaints were high, especially when they got requests to return books for which only call numbers were given. Complainers would come in or phone, and a librarian would have to look up the book for them--a procedure that was as time-wasting as it was annoying.

The problem was solved by adaptation. Whenever an inquiry was made as to the title of a recalled book, or whenever a recalled book was returned with the notice, the title (which had just been looked up or was right in front of the librarian) was entered into the record.

Like most adaptive systems, this one adjusted *the most frequently accessed records* first. Therefore, complaints were reduced dramatically once the first few hundred high-usage books were updated. The *majority* of books in the library remain unconverted to title information after several years. Still, complaints diminished almost to zero, because those untitled books are essentially never used, or at least never returned late. Thus, not only was the conversion effort spread painlessly over a long time, but it was at least cut in half because half the books will *never* be converted.

After several years of using this system, the librarians were able to tell (from lack of title information) which books were the most likely candidates for eliminating from the collection, or placing in "warehouse" storage.

SHARING ADAPTATION

Sometimes, part of the adaptation burden can be placed on the human beings involved. In one information accessing application, only a single individual was authorized to see information in each record. Since inquiries were made by telephone, it was just possible that someone could discover the inquiry key (such as the birthdate in the savings bank application), and continue to make inquiries without detection. Although nobody knew if this was a real danger, certain users were apprehensive.

To reduce their fears, the system was modified to retain a *count* of the number of previous inquiries. When a successful inquiry was made over the phone, the operator would, on demand, give this number to the customer. The customer could then be satisfied that nobody had made an inquiry since the last one he made himself. Because the count could only increase, it was impossible to make an on-line inquiry without it being detected--provided the user kept track of his last inquiry number.

Like many adaptive systems, this one bothered only the users who were concerned with the aspect it protected. Other users didn't even know of its existence, but could be told if they expressed anxiety-- and even given the current number so they might be able to figure out if someone had already been accessing their account. As a byproduct of this system, the system managers were able to know the frequency of telephone inquiries into various classes of account.

So far, nobody has been caught making illegal inquiries, but that may merely mean the system is working very well indeed--*preventing* leaks rather than *plugging* them.

THE FUTURE OF ADAPTATION

An adaptive system absorbs real world information from its normal interaction with its users. What could be more natural? More appealing to our sense of good system design? Why, then, do some designers fear to specify even the simplest adaptive mechanisms?

LACK OF CERTAINTY

Many designers were attracted to computer systems because they present a sense of precision and infallibility (especially when described by hardware salespeople). How comforting, in this confusing world, to find *something* that appears to be completely precise and accurate. To such people, the input side of the business has always been a nemesis--an ugly duckling in a flock of lovely swans. Ideas like "self-checking" numbers have great appeal to these people, because they give the illusion of certainty amidst confusion.

Adaptive checking cannot approach this promise (false though it be) of certainty. For one thing, self-checking numbers can be applied only to *assigned identifiers*, which they hope point to *one precise record*. No checking of *quantities*, or *patterns*, could ever promise one-for-one certainty. It can promise only to observe the environment and approve situations that seem "reasonable." For those who demand the illusion of certainty, such reasonable behavior is insufficient. It is, moreover, to be feared.

SECOND-ORDER CERTAINTY

Adaptive checking schemes start by assuming that no designer can predict the future with certainty. Certainty is only for gods and fools. Yet even though we can't know the future in detail, we can know much in a "second order" fashion. That is, we may know, with high probability, the general structure of the future, but not the precise values of the parameters that characterize that structure. Adaptive systems allow the system *itself* to study the inexact future as it unfolds, within a general structure laid down by the designer.

"But," cries the anxious designer, lusting after first-order certainty, "adaptation depends upon *chance*. What if we get a few unlucky inputs that cause an improper adaptation?" To this fear, the best reply is the words of Sir Ronald Fisher (1958)--written when countering a similar objection to adaptation through natural selection:

> *The income derived from a Casino by its proprietor may, in one sense, be said to depend upon a succession of favourable chances, although the phrase contains a suggestion of improbability more appropriate to the hopes of the patrons of his establishment.*

Any system interacting with this imperfect, mortal world depends upon chance. Isn't it better, then, to design our systems so that we are on the proprietor's side of the table?

USE OF RESOURCES

Even designers with no fear of uncertainty are often dismayed at the "extra" resources consumed by adaptive schemes, or, for that matter, by any scheme that increases reliability. Such designers blanch when they hear that "over 50% of IMS code is reported to be for integrity and recovery." To add bit strings, character strings, and count upon count to each data record seems, to them, to be hanging a millstone around the neck of their "efficient" systems design.

They overlook the trend--no, the tidal wave--of lower priced storage devices with ever greater capacities. In many cases, they design as if the disk drive had never been invented, let alone refined several thousandfold--and then surpassed. In terms of present resources, the adaptive schemes presented here consume essentially nothing at all--and pay back any consumption many times over.

Indeed, if we take a more general view, there is reason to believe that our adaptive schemes are far too simple and conservative. A slight familiarity with biological systems and successful man-made systems will demonstrate the depth of a remark by von Neumann (1966):

> *If you look at automata which have been built by men or which exist in nature you will very frequently notice that their structure is controlled to a much larger extent by the manner in which they might fail and by the (more or less effective) precautionary measures which have been taken against their failure.*

In biological systems, redundancy is so high that 99% or more of all resources are devoted to it. For example, in the human brain any individual cell can die without noticeable effect. Indeed, in many cases, large chunks of brain matter can be excised without detectable influence on behavior.

It may be the immaturity of our computer systems that makes them so *insufficiently redundant*. In the future, we can hopefully expect them to grow more and more like biological systems--not in details of construction, but in general principles. And one of the most general principles of biology is to protect the system against failure, or to minimize the cost of a failure--*whatever resources it takes*. Adaptive systems do that. Resources so used are well spent.

HUMANENESS

Adaptive systems take a gentle view of humanity. Users need not possess godlike perfection. They can, at times, be untrustworthy, disloyal, harmful, un- friendly, rude, cruel, disobedient, gloomy, prodigal, fearful, messy, and irreverent. Rigid, non-adaptive systems falter in the face of these human foibles, but adaptive systems muddle through. More than that, self- adjusting systems remember that people like to be treated with respect, courtesy, and assistance.

Any user has the right to know why the computer is shouting ERROR at him, and not have to make unin- formed guesses. Users have the right to be respected for their knowledge of the real world, and the right to adjust the standards set on the quality of their work. After all, *they* are ultimately responsible-- not the computer.

If the designer accepts these human principles, self-adjustment makes his job easier. He need not make impossibly detailed guesses about the future-- such as reasonable limits for order quantities for 50,000 products. He simply designs an adaptive system that will derive the limits for itself. Then, as a byproduct, the system will tell him the answers it derives.

BYPRODUCTS

Adaptive systems *always* yield byproduct inform- ation, because they must be designed to keep track of their own performance. Some common byproducts include:

equifinal behavior with minimum startup cost

frequency information on classes of transactions

more meaningful sharing of responsibilities be- tween people and machines

more reasonable detection and correction, which tends to diminish the number of outrageous errors emanating from the system

In many instances, the "byproducts" prove more significant than the "main product" of an adaptive approach.

In the final analysis, the principal byproduct of any adaptive design is to cushion "future shock." Toffler has popularized the view that change processes are impinging on human society at a faster rate and to a greater degree than ever before in history. Toffler and other "futurists" have suggested that we need more adaptive mechanisms to cope with this mushrooming change.

The designers of adaptive systems will observe change in action every day--through the system's monitoring facilities. In the past, these changes were perceivable only when they "suddenly" switched from quantitative to qualitative--when they became a "shock." From their exposure to manageable change, these designers should acquire a vital new perspective--a new set of priorities. If they don't, there won't be any future shock, because there won't be any future.

A SUMMARY OF EXPECTED ATTRIBUTES

The following is a simplified multidimensional view of the normal attributes which the designer can expect when specifying some kind of adaptive checking. The designer must calculate or otherwise estimate the more accurate attributes for his particular implementation in order to compare this option against other design alternatives.

PRODUCTIVITY

Input operators using on-line terminals can achieve greater productivity rates than with other methods with comparable checking capabilities, because checking is automatically tuned to require operator intervention in truly exceptional cases. Other methods demand compromises between detection capability and operator interaction, because limits and patterns cannot economically be set for individual cases.

When using adaptive initialization, keying rate

may decrease to enter new or exceptional data which
the programs have determined are missing from the system, yet are needed at the time. Here, the real productivity saving is in not having to gather data in
advance for which the system has no current use--and,
in some cases, may *never* have any use. Compared with
systems which gather "all" data in advance, the productivity of the input operation is multiplied many
times. Even in the long run, and in those systems
that will eventually capture "all" data, much of the
work has been done as a "free" byproduct of a related
operational work process, with no measurable effect on
that process. If, in addition, there are data which
are *never* needed (like the titles of unused books in
the library data base), there can be savings up to
perhaps 75% of the work that would have otherwise been
expended.

RELIABILITY

Any reasonably designed adaptive limit or pattern
checking will, by the nature of the system, provide
more reliable accepted data than a system with fixed
limits or patterns. More important, perhaps, is that
even when inaccurate values *are* accepted, they will be
more *reasonable* than those accepted by fixed systems,
and so less costly and disruptive.

In addition to detecting errors in keying or in
source document interpretation, adaptive limit or pattern checking can catch errors made at any time in
passing from source to system, such as from the following (see Gilb, 1973, "Error Sources"):

misplacing decimal points

wrong writing of numbers

using the wrong field on a form

using the wrong positions in a field

terminal failures

communication line failures

operating system or application program bugs

Checking done immediately prior to use--such as up-dating an inventory or financial account--gives better protection than controls at an early point, after which data can be corrupted.

It is also worth noting that evolutionary updat-ing or initialization of files is likely to result in higher quality data than advance mass collection and validation. At the time of evolutionary registration, the subject is most probably at hand in some original form--personally, on the telephone, on a letterhead, in the book in front of you, and so forth. Therefore, the data are more likely to be current, accurate, and verifiable--more so, at least, than data pulled from old, inaccurate, and unverifiable files or records.

PORTABILITY

Adaptive checking systems require no special hard-ware except perhaps larger *capacity* in computing and secondary storage. Therefore, they should be movable unless capacity is downgraded. On the other hand, they can be extremely portable to different *environ-ments*, since no special effort need be made to set the checking values characteristic of the new environment. The new system can either be started from just where the old system was, or from a "neutral" state. After a short time, it will have "forgotten" its origins and be in the same equifinal state, adapted to the new environment.

IMPLEMENTATION EASE

Contrary to the impression many people have, adaptive systems can be particularly simple to implem-ent, for their essence is to let the system do the work. There is probably no other way to get compar-able checking efficiency with so little implementation effort. Also, an adaptive initialization will be feasible for an otherwise conventional system, such as the phone number checking in the savings bank.

HARDWARE RESOURCES

Adaptive methods require secondary storage resources which vary in fairly direct proportion to the number and degree of such techniques applied. This storage is for the experience data which serves as the necessary background for making changes which improve the process--as when adjusting a limit check.

The programs to create and to use this experiential data will occupy primary memory space, although much of it is exception logic that will reside in virtual storage. The amount of such storage and of corresponding processor time will depend on the complexity of the self-adapting tasks actually designed into the system.

For the present, in systems such as sketched here, the amount of this resource will probably be trivial, and likely to be paid for in obvious savings in other hardware resources. In the future, the inevitable expansion of this concept to large, complex, long-term systems will doubtlessly lead to a significant portion of program logic and storage space being devoted to adaptive purposes. Gilb (1972) has proposed an overall design strategy for data base management founded on this principle, where the primary objective is efficient long-term use of both hardware and human resources.

SECURITY

Several examples have been given of adaptive checking to implement security schemes. In general, security of this type is based on the idea that any striking deviation from past experience needs to be called to someone's attention. This may be a one-time deviation, or a long-term repetition of one particular and peculiar pattern. Either type of violation can be detected by suitable adaptive schemes, especially if they are properly instrumented so that no one person has the sole access to the fact of an interaction.

Further protection is provided by "random" sampling, which adds to the unpredictability of the system from the point of view of a would-be penetrator, and thus serves to discourage *attempts* at penetration.

EXTENDABILITY

Adaptive checking need have no effect at all on the input format used, so has no effect at all on extendability in that dimension. As for system *growth*, adaptive schemes generally have the interesting property that they work *better* the larger the volume of input. The sampling of the environment is then smoother, and the "law of large numbers" may help out.

On the other hand, if we *mix* two essentially different environments, the system will have trouble adapting effectively. A few large customers, for instance, can invalidate limit checking for all small customers. A single customer with odd ordering patterns can decrease the effectiveness of pattern checking for everyone else. To some extent, these effects can be overcome by setting up subcategories to *partition* the environment.

DESIGN EXERCISES

1. Reexamine the first exercise of the previous chapter (page 191) to see if further improvement in the design can be achieved through the use of some form of adaptive checking. Discuss how adaptive checking affected the performance of the design, and if not, why not.

2. Consider the creation of some "master" file you have experienced, and list some of the costs and difficulties encountered in the creation. Design a different approach to creating the file--one that uses some sort of adaptation to overcome such costs and difficulties. Estimate the savings your design would have made.

3. In some input application with which you are

familiar, obtain a long series of quantitative inputs for 3 or 4 different "items." Using these inputs to simulate the environment, model a pattern checking system to measure how effective it would be at detecting errors; how many false alarms it would give for each correct detection; and how much interaction would be needed to keep it operating. Using these figures, make a cost-benefit analysis for installing such a system in this application.

4. The straightforward method of keeping a running mean value involves accumulating the total values (t) and the total number of values (n). As time goes on, both t and n grow large, and the mean will be almost impossible to change. In effect, this method keeps the history of the quantity *forever*.

If we are to keep the mean responsive to recent experience, there must be some method of "aging" the values. One method is to *halve* t and n every month, or other convenient period. Thus, if the total orders had been 10,000 for 100 orders, for an average of 100, t and n would become 5,000 and 50. Although the average would not change, the *response* of the averaging procedure to a new value would be different.

For instance, a new order of 1,000 items would make the old values 11,000 and 101, for a mean of 109, while the new, halved quantities would become 6,000 and 51, for a mean of 117. To the extent that the new large order reflects an actual change in the environment, the larger value will be a better reflection of increased limits on checking.

Explore the behavior of such systems of aging, perhaps with a computer simulation. Discuss how parameters would be set for various operational environments. Discuss also how currently available information, such as might be accumulated for sales analyses, can be used in such a system--or, conversely, how the information from such a system can be used to monitor other interesting facts.

5. The system in the previous problem is closely related to the technique called *exponential smoothing*. Repeat the problem for the exponential smoothing

technique, and compare the two techniques according to their design attributes.

6.   If limit-checking limits are adjusted upwards and never readjusted, they can be expected to grow without decreasing, according to the largest acceptable quantity experienced to date.   Under many circumstances, the "largest quantity experienced so far" tends to grow as the logarithm of time.   A notable example is "the largest flood stage ever experienced so far," which is evidently important in designing dams.

Reexamine the data used in Exercise 3, with an eye to determining how "the largest quantity experienced so far" tends to grow in those data.   Discuss the implications of this growth pattern for monitoring the performance of the system over time, as with management reports on unusual events.   For a reference, see Gumbel (1958).

Chapter VIII

Tolerating Variance

"He remarked to me then," said that mildest of men,
    "'If your Snark be a Snark, that is right:
Fetch it home by all means--you may serve it with greens,
    And it's handy for striking a light.'"

"'You may seek it with thimbles--and seek it with care;
    You may hunt it with forks and hope;
You may threaten its life with a railway-share;
    You may charm it with smiles and soap--'"

("That's exactly the method," the Bellman bold
    In a hasty parenthesis cried,
"That's exactly the way I have always been told
    That the capture of Snarks should be tried!")

--*The Hunting of the Snark, Fit the Third*

In short, the "exact" way to hunt a Snark is not "exactly" anything at all--it is a great variety of methods, any one of which might achieve the capture of the elusive (and, oh beamish nephew, dangerous) Snark. And fortunate it is, too, for ill-fated Baker is, like most of us, an extremely variable person. If he was allowed no variation, he would *never* capture a Snark. If you don't believe this, try hunting some Snark of an input to some Boojum of an operating system that allows *one and only one RIGHT* form of expression.

To be human is to vary, and to tolerate variance in others. Shall we make our people more mechanical, or our machines more human? Or, at least, Snarklike?

DESIGN FOR VARIATION

When trying to sell a computer, we stress the enormous "flexibility" arising from "the stored program concept." Once the machine arrives, however, we begin to emphasize neatness, precision, and strict adherence to the computer's rules.

Somewhere between dream and realization, all that potential flexibility has been lost. To the uninitiated, a "computer" is a device that *must* have one precise form for each input. This impression is so strong and so inhuman that we see nubile women and virile men wearing T-shirts that plead:

I AM A HUMAN BEING

PLEASE DO NOT FOLD, SPINDLE, OR MUTILATE

Yet to us computer folk, such cries of alarm are baffling--and stimulate defensive responses. "Don't those outsiders know of the great flexibility of the computer with its stored program concept? Of course, we don't actually *use* any of that flexibility--that would be too costly to program. It's much cheaper to have 220,000,000 people write their last names first than to program a computer to read them the other way around. Why can't people just learn to do things the way that's easiest for us to program? Then we could devote ourselves to using the great flexibility of the computer!"

LEVELS OF VARIATION

Let's begin by acknowledging that it *is* more convenient for computers if the *internal* data forms are precisely specified and adhered to. Let's also acknowledge that it *used to be expensive* to allow for variation on input. But let's also acknowledge that the *cost of not allowing input variation* is far, far greater than most other costs in many systems. Then we can start asking *sensible* design questions--questions that compare the cost of variation with the benefits.

Once we have made this sensible beginning, the outlines of the variation problem begin to sharpen. The first step is to recognize that not all variation is the same--either in cost or in benefit. From the computer's point of view, there are several levels of input variation, depending on what efforts are needed to make the information internally useable:

> *Some forms can be interpreted correctly without the slightest doubt, even though there are several alternative forms.*
>
> *Some forms can be interpreted by simple program logic, in spite of their irregularity, though they may be subject to stricter review or auditing later on in the process.*
>
> *Some forms are interpretable with such doubt that the program should refuse to continue until human judgement is applied to supplement the program.*
>
> *Some are not intelligible in any useful way (though improving the program might change that classification) and are rejected with suitable diagnostics for human handling away from the machine.*
>
> *Some are intelligible, but as the* wrong *thing.*

DESIGN APPROACHES

The rigid systems that typify computers to the general public are a result of faulty design thinking. Designers of these systems have acted as if there were only two sorts of input--right and wrong. At best, a third class is added--wrong, so stop processing and send it back. Change for the better is possible, but only if we incorporate variation tolerance into our typical design process:

> *Start by establishing requirements, such as cost,*

reliability, and flexibility.

Analyze the existing human, organizational, and computer environment to establish the normal patterns of message communication. Determine what codes and sequences are natural, but don't stop there. Also determine what variations are normal, and what level they are to the computer.

Because we are designing for variance, it is neither necessary nor desirable to find all the answers. In fact, it's not even possible, so why try? Instead, design the system to adapt easily to new variations--an approach that will succeed even if the original system is quite rigid in what it will accept, since everything changes anyway--except change itself.

Initially, design sets of messages which cater to the most common variations. Allow for manual specification to handle further exceptions. But keep everything under programmed control, even if it isn't fully automated, so the system can provide information for further improvement--and so the system can be changed internally without changing the way it appears to its users.

IS THE TOLERANCE REAL?

Some of our readers will respond to this approach by remarking, "Oh, we *already* do that! Our systems have always been designed to allow variation." We hope they're right. Most claims for tolerant systems are based on *calling* them tolerant, not *making* them tolerant.

To illustrate this "naming" approach, consider the "design" of the job control input for IBM operating systems. The format of a job control statement is the sequence of fields:

//name operation operand comment

To quote from the *Job Control Language Reference Manual*, Order Number GC28-6704-2, page 39:

Control statement fields--except for the name

field, which must begin in column 3--can be coded
in free form. Free form means that the fields
need not begin in a particular column. Separate
each field with a blank; the blank serves as a
delimiter between fields.

This cheery statement about "free form" leads the
unwary novice down the primrose path. Perhaps he
should take warning from the *obviously* imprecise statement, "Separate each field with a blank." It should
have said, "Separate two fields from one another with
a blank." But this is only the beginning. At great
pain and expense, the user will discover (if he sticks
with it) that "free form" means:

> free to put *almost* any number of blanks between
> these fields

> *not* free to put any blanks *within* a field (which
> would indeed separate the field)

> *not* free to use positions 73-80 of the 80-posit-
> ion record

> *not* free to use position 72 except for one spec-
> ial purpose

> *not* free to put too many blanks between fields so
> that certain fields start too far to the right

The earlier manuals didn't even mention the name field
exception. User complaints about the misleading use
of the term "free form" led to this change, after
which the manual writers must have thought that *now*
they truly had "free form" commands. It all sounds a
bit like some peoples' interpretation of "free speech":
you're free to say anything--except what might make a
difference politically.

Even if *all* the exceptions are described in the
manual, does this excellent documentation make up for
a junky system? Wouldn't it be better to forget about
"free form" and simply tell the user there is a rigid
set of rules he'd better obey to the letter? That's
what hundreds of instructors have finally done, when
trying to teach this inhuman input system.

But this system is *doubly* obnoxious. Where variation *is* tolerated, it's *not the variation the user*

wants! Instead, it's whatever the programmers thought they could supply for minimal programming cost. *None* of the design steps we've outlined were followed, which is *not* what we mean by designing for variation tolerance.

SEQUENCE TOLERANCE

The computer's ability to process data in any convenient sequence is not reflected in the majority of current input designs. In addition to its "free form" problems, the IBM operating system job control language is a typical case of sequence *intolerance*. Although explicitly identified parts of fields can be in varied sequences, other parts must be in a rigidly prescribed order. Even worse, the commands themselves must be in a rigid sequence--defined with respect to the sequence of other commands not readily visible.

THE FORM-FILLING SYMPTOM

In spite of the inadequacies of the job control language, IBM is probably well ahead of current practice in variation tolerance. In a typical commercial installation, many input items are *manually* copied onto preprinted forms. "Form-filling"--this hideously unnatural act--has become synonymous with oppressive bureaucracy. Oppressive? Yes, oppressive, but sheepishly accepted by millions--none of whom realize that this slavish work could be substantially simplified or eliminated through variation tolerant designs.

A form is nothing but a manual device for formatting, sequencing, and coding for computers. Cost considerations alone dictate that we eliminate this medieval practice, leaving the formatting, sequencing, and coding to the computer itself.

All computers have memory. *All* computers can resequence items in that memory--much more cheaply and accurately than human beings can resequence items on paper. Therefore, when a designer sees someone filling in a form merely to resequence, he is seeing *the symptom of a disease*--a costly, error-prone disease that attacks not only the data preparation, but every other aspect of the system.

NATURAL SEQUENCES

Wherever the designer finds form-filling, he finds a starting place for "establishing the normal patterns of message communication." If the form-filling requires resequencing, some "natural" sequence is being rearranged for the computer's convenience. The designer might allow that natural sequence as a variation to the computers "natural" sequence--one for us and one for them. Similarly, where there is no resequencing, or no form-filling at all, the designer should take care to *preserve* the sequences involved.

Once a natural sequence has been discovered, the designer must decide whether to allow variant sequences. Certain sequences are so natural to their users that little is to be gained from allowing variation. Indeed, allowing a little variation may only serve to confuse the users, as we saw in the example of IBM's job control language.

In the international book trade, for example, the product description sequence

quantity author(if any) title

is so ingrained that we would be foolish to allow other sequences. To do so, we would have to add identifying information, for self-identification will not generally be possible. Consider the case

10   DAVID COPPERFIELD,   CHARLES DICKENS

Is this an order for 10 copies of the famous novel? Or is it for a biography of Mr. Dickens by a Mr. Copperfield?

We must demand sequence in some applications, unless we are willing to try something worse. We will have to evaluate the importance of sequence tolerance against the disadvantages of such an input format as:

10 T:DAVID COPPERFIELD A:CHARLES DICKENS

Before fixing any design decisions, the analyst should consider the natural working habits of the people who *first* record the source data. The accepted sequence of *trained professional* personnel may not correspond to the feelings of trainees or casual users. First generation computer people will swear that

COPPERFIELD, DAVID

is the *natural* way to give a person's name. People not afflicted with this occupational disease would be hard pressed to agree with them, unless they happen to be named JEROME JEROME JEROME.

ITEM ORDER

The designer's goal should be a system that captures data items in the same sequences in which they occur. Normally, there are simple ways of permitting this much sequence tolerance within a message, though there will undoubtedly be situations in which this goal must be balanced against other system goals. As a rule, however, such unstructured situations as letters, supplier invoices, accounting input documents from outside sources, salesperson orders, telephone operator notes, and items originating in the plant or warehouse will greatly benefit from a measure of sequence tolerance within a message.

Moreover, sequence variations within a short message are usually easy to handle--unless the designer makes the mistake of coding all data elements into numbers.

MESSAGE ORDER

Sequence variations *among* messages potentially represent a larger data processing problem, especially in their demands on primary storage space. In order to process a complete set of messages, the system will have to store variable-length tables of messages in primary and, ultimately, in secondary memory. To make matters worse, some popular high level languages are not sufficiently high for such programming problems.

Even so, nothing in this programming task should prove insurmountable for junior programmers--especially if they are aided by a clever virtual storage system to cope with the backing store logic.

In looking for potential system improvements through message-order tolerance, the designer listens for someone saying, "This message *must* come first, because all other messages depend on it." If all other messages depend on it, then the *computer* can hold them until it arrives. Programming this waiting function should prove less difficult than programming the checking function to be sure the crucial message *is* first, and chastizing the operator if it isn't.

For example, a large number of individual details on an international invoice certainly depend on the destination country. Nevertheless, if people want to enter the country code later rather than sooner, all dependent messages can patiently wait, rather than forcing people to change their inclinations, habits, or conventions. There *might* be factors we've overlooked that make their choice a profitable one. No designer is omniscient.

GROUPS OF MESSAGES

One such external factor is the need for *error correction*. We've already seen the usefulness of resynchronization for individual messages and parts of messages. The same need often exists across a large group of messages. Frequently, the "message" has been defined in relation to computer needs, rather than human feelings about what information naturally travels together.

In many applications, a group of messages (such as the items on an order blank) are related in the operator's mind. A late item might spur the realization that an earlier item was wrong. Holding such a related group in memory until the entire group is complete has a number of advantages:

Files are not updated until the finality of the transaction is assured. This facilitates error recovery and simplifies programming by eliminating backtracking.

Many more internal consistency checks become possible.

More flexibility in the message design is permitted, because each transaction can be gathered internally from several messages, thus breaking the "one-message/one-transaction" coupling.

Given appropriate video devices, the entire group can be fed back to the operator for overall scanning before the transactions are registered. Reformatting can reveal inconsistencies that the computer would be hard pressed to discover, but which the operator can see at a glance.

Feeding back the entire group permits the operator to check that the variations lead to the proper end result, thus encouraging confident use of variational forms, for more comfort and fewer errors.

Processing messages in groups carries certain risks along with these advantages--risks which must be addressed by the designer:

On-the-spot corrections must still be permitted, on both an item and a message basis.

Global corrections may require more feedback to ensure correct application. Although reformatting can be useful, it may also be necessary to save each transaction in its original form--not some decoded form--for feedback.

Trying to fix up an entire collection of messages may prove to be a divergent process, with each correction producing another error or two. Limits should be put on patchwork, in order to help the operator out of such fruitless loops.

CONTENT TOLERANCE

The same sort of analysis and design thinking applies to the *content* of messages as to the sequence of items or messages. It is most often cheaper to program acceptance of frequently occuring "natural" codes and variations than to teach employees to write the "correct" codes. When dealing with the "public"--that is, with people who don't make their living keying data into a computer--there really isn't much alternative, for to do otherwise is to court rebellion, sabotage, and other "people problems."

TYPES OF VARIATION

We can conveniently recognize 3 types of variation in content:

SYNONYMS, where there is a small set of alternative names or forms for the same item, and there are a small number of items so that the alternatives may conveniently be listed. Or, if the number of items is large, the synonyms might be obtained by an adaptive initialization, as in the previous chapter.

GRAMMARS, where the set of alternatives is large, but can be described precisely by a compact set of grammatical descriptors, such as a formal grammar.

OPEN-ENDED SETS, where there is no clear and concise rule for specifying the allowable variations, and in fact there may be a fuzzy idea of just how much tolerance can be tolerated.

STANDARD VARIATION RECOGNIZERS

Synonyms are trivial to handle by a program, if we are willing to allocate enough storage for a "dictionary." Certainly for common synonym situations, such as dates (which we have already discussed), or time, or money, or quantity, we can develop rather compact subroutines which can become "standard variation recognizers" for all of our programs. This kind of standard will improve the lot of operators, programmers, and all people who use the system, at a cost that will be amortized over a long period.

For instance, it should be simple to produce a subroutine for recognizing all these common variants:

TIME WORKED: 7.5 HR, 1 SHIFT, 1 DAY, 7HR/30MIN,

7:30, 450MIN, 450min, 450Min.

MONEY: 5.00,   5$, $5, $5.00,   005.00

.53,   53¢,   ¢53, $0.53

$5,389.27,   5389.27,   5,389.27$

QUANTITY: 234567.89   234,567.89   +2.345E+5

234.5THOU   234.567,89
*(The last item is needed if Europ-
ean and American operators use the
same system.)*

Another useful subroutine is one that recognizes simple *plurals*, or, rather, attempts to transform an unrecognizable noun into a singular form that might be recognized. Over 90% of English plurals are formed by adding "s" or "es"--so there is no excuse for a system that accepts BOLT and doesn't accept BOLTS, or accepts BOXES but punishes the operator who asks for BOX.

Once again, 100% performance is not required. Nobody really expects a system--even a system for ordering toy animals--to recognize PLATYPII, or PLATYPUSSIES, as plurals of PLATYPUS, or MONGEESE as plural of MONGOOSE. Similarly, if there is any doubt about the correct recognition, the system can simply *ask*-- if it's on-line--for operator confirmation.

The standard variation recognizers can use a grammar, a short synonym list, or a combination of both-- it's strictly a matter of programming technique. We can have acceptance lists or rejection lists, acceptance grammars or rejection grammars. We can apply the list first or the grammar first, or have a sequence of lists and/or grammars to classify an input item. A standard variation recognizer is essentially a *compiler* with a trivial "code generation" or "semantic" phase. A great body of literature exists on compiler writing (see, for example, Gries, 1971, or Wilcox, in press) for the designer to study. Fortunately, the syntactic, or recognizer, part of the compiling

process is the best understood part, and that will be
all that's needed for input purposes.

SYNONYM LISTS

There is one special standard variation recognizer that works for all cases, if we are willing to allocate sufficient storage. This recognizer, of course,
is a dictionary, or table. Where usage is irregular,
or not standard enough to justify programming a special recognizer, there still may be sources of plausible variations in such places as telephone books,
catalogs, or indices. The mere existence of *cross-
references* in such sources is a good indication that
we might profitably allow for variation.

For example, these are cases found in public
sources:

NAME	SYNONYM	SOURCE
SAS	SCANDINAVIAN AIRLINES	*Telephone book*
RCA COMPUTERS	UNIVAC, SPERRY	*Telephone book*
CURTAINS	DRAPERIES, VALENCES, SHADES	*Catalog*
FOOTWEAR	SHOES, BOOTS, SLIPPERS, PUMPS	*Catalog*
PUMP	SHOE	*Index*
PUMP	IRRIGATOR	*Index*

ADAPTIVE LISTS

The computer can acquire a synonym list adaptively. New items are added to the list whenever the operator confirms that a new form is equivalent to an old
one. Gradually, Zipf's Law will take over and the average interaction will be shortened.

The operator can also realize the promise of
Zipf's Law. If the system presents a shorter synonym
each time a long variant is chosen, the operator will

learn synonyms rather rapidly. True, rarely used
terms will not be learned, but the rare use of a long
form will not have much effect on the average length.

Even when no synonyms are presented, adaptation
will take place if there is enough regularity in abbreviation for the users to adapt without feedback. In
an informal study of the operating systems for the IBM
360/370, the length of commands to the system had a
high inverse correlation (-.83) with the amount of
operator experience with the system. The abbreviation
method was simple--the initial character of the comm-
and could be used, as in M for MOUNT or R for REPLY.
More experienced operators used the single character
forms more frequently, for a net reduction in interaction time, as well as in typing errors such as REPYL
for REPLY.

A third kind of adaptation can occur, though not
always automatically, after the system has gained experience with synonym lists. By monitoring these
lists, and their usage, the designer can call for programming changes that substitute formal grammars or
other explicit code for part of a list--thus achieving
faster operation and/or less memory consumed.

For a large "dictionary," it may be advantageous
to reorganize periodically for faster access, just as
we would with any other file. If recent frequency of
reference to each entry is tabulated, and if the dictionary is referenced by "hashing," it may pay to re-
create the entire dictionary, putting the most frequent entries in first. In this way, the most common
forms will be accessed in the shortest time, because
they will most often be in their home address. Such
a system is adaptive in its efficiency, as well as in
its effectiveness.

SPELLING

Typing REPYL for REPLY shouldn't be a serious error in a well-designed operating system. The number
of commands is so small that simple transposition errors could be corrected by a variety of techniques.
More general spelling errors, such as "pelet" for

"pellet," or "recieve" for "receive," can be corrected through a stored dictionary of misspellings. Such a dictionary can be found in secretarial handbooks, or could be accumulated adaptively.

Other types of "spelling" errors fall into distinct patterns, and so can be corrected by rather simple procedures. Here is a partial list that illustrates some of the minor variations that would be considered errors in most systems, but which we suggest as candidates for programmed tolerance and correct interpretation (see Gilb, 1976, for further examples):

Out of several letters in a data element, one or two letters are entirely wrong.

Two letters are transposed (RECIEVE for RECEIVE).

Double letters are made single, or vice versa (SWANSSON or SWANSON; KAUFMAN, KAUFFMANN, KAUFMANN, or KAUFFMAN).

National equivalents or other variants in different languages are used (GENEVA, GENEVE, GENF, or GINIVRA; FLAVOR or FLAVOUR; PARK or PARC).

Spoken words are misunderstood (GILB, JILB, JYLB, or GILLDE; BINGHAMTON, BIGHAMTON, BIRMINGHAMTON, BINGHAMPTON, BINGHAMDEN, BINGHAMILTON, BINGHATTEN, BINGHADDON, BIGHAMMOND, or BINGAMDON--all of which have been recognized by the U.S. Postal Service as BINGHAMTON!).

Written letters are unclear (I for l, "/", and "one"; O for 0, C, and Q; Z for 2, S, and 5).

Abbreviations are taken more or less at random (JOHN for JOHNATHON, or J, J., JON, JOHNNY, and JONNY--should we take JACK?).

The designer's traditional reaction to such problems was to increase training, motivation, standardization, discipline, recruitment standards, improve forms, or eliminate the human element entirely--in short, to go against all knowledge of the psychology of errors. As George Bernard Shaw said, "Anyone who can spell in English can't be very bright."

Shaw's remark takes on new meaning when we

consider that computers (which aren't very bright at
all) can now spell better than most humans. For those
who don't believe that assertion, we recommend a study
of the literature on spelling correction by computer,
such as Morgan's (1970) paper.

What a blissful idiot the computer is, doing exactly what it is told, neither more nor less. But
people...ah, people! No matter how much we try to
force rules upon them, they won't be as cooperative as
the computer. No, it's worse than that. The *more*
we try to force rules on them, the *less* they cooperate.
If we command them not to fold, spindle, or mutilate,
it only gives them new ideas of how to retaliate for
inhuman treatment. In a data entry department, we may
get away with *some* inhumanity by sheer despotism
threatening even worse. With the general public,
facism won't work. Isn't it time we tried the most
obvious yet most ignored technique--tolerance?

SOUND SEARCHING

Satisfactory solutions to the problems of variant
forms can be programmed within the framework of general subroutines. A typical example deals with the
correction of sound errors--for which there are a number of commercially available systems. Internally,
the US Bureau of Immigration and Naturalization classifies immigrants according to the sound of their names,
using the following algorithm:

Vowels are ignored entirely.

Double letters are made single.

*Letters in one "group" are made into the same
letter. The groups used are:*

BPFVW

RL

MN

DT

CKQSZX

GJ

In this system, a trivial algorithm turns WALLACE, VALACHI, and WILLIS into the same "key"--BRC. Such a key can then be used to access an index of possible candidates. Not all cases can be recognized correctly the first time, so that a certain degree of human interaction in 1-3% of the cases should be expected. But the most common and interesting variations can be found by searching the indices according to *several* such key transformations--the number of transformations being adjusted by the designer to yield the requisite level of first-time indentification.

HELP FROM CONTEXT

In some situations, other data may be brought into the decision. In a retail telephone ordering system, we may have an order from a Mr. NORTON, which we cannot find precisely in our file. The transformed key under the simple phonetic system yields 3 possibilities:

MORTON   NORDEN   MARDIAN

which are then resolved by noting that the 3 telephone numbers in the records were

488-9126 465-2153 432-8434

and the call back number given on the phone was

465-2135

or so the operator thought. The entire process is illustrated in Figure 8.1.

Similarly, in an accounts receivable situation, the amount of payment that exactly matches one and only one of the candidate accounts is likely to be a reliable clue to choosing among them.

The logic of reliable recognition is straightforward, but requires some imagination. Look at what people do. Think about how you search the telephone directory for the scribbled name of a friend you met at last night's party. These actions will give you an idea of how to proceed. Above all, don't overcomplicate the problem. Allow for a small percentage of

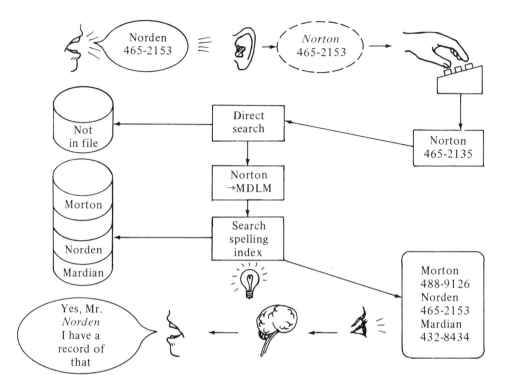

Figure 8.1   Using sound-searching and context information to obtain a correct record
in the presence of a variety of errors.

human-machine interaction, and don't go overboard in
the quest for a "perfect" system.

PROCEDURE TOLERANCE

When psychological researchers are designing a new experiment, both the ethical and scientific precedents
dictate that the experimenter himself be the first
"victim." If this precaution were universally adopted
by the input design profession, we probably wouldn't
have to say anything about procedure tolerance. The
experience would do a better job than we could hope for.

WHAT ABOUT STRUCTURE?

For some reason, control procedures tend to be

the most rigid part of any input system--perhaps because they so closely follow program control logic.
Softening the control seems to require wishy-washy
programming, which nobody wants in these days when
"structure" is the watchword.

But if "structure" means anything, it means the
structure of the *entire* system. By including a greater ability to handle common input variations, we may
apparently make the program structure more complex.
Even if this were true, the structure of the *total*
data handling system is brought under far better control by the elimination of unnecessary manual complications. Most of the problems can be fit under the
same roof, if only the roof is high enough.

USEFUL SUBROUTINES

A few simple techniques can soften control logic
immeasurably without compromising program structure in
any way at all. For example, procedures can be added
to the library which

make it easy to write prompting messages, as in

CALL OBTAIN_INPUT('YES', 'NO', 'HELP');

*which prompts that there are three acceptable
replies*

*make it easy to specify alternative equivalent
replies, as in*

IF INPUT_IS('YES', 'Y', 'OKAY', 'OK', 'AGREE',...)

*or in the form with the alternatives in a varia-
ble-length list, such as*

IF INPUT_IS(YES_INPUT_LIST) THEN ...

*make it easy to add to the lists of acceptable
replies as in the handling of non-standard inputs
with*

ELSE CALL INTERACTIVE_LIST_UPDATE;

*which, under some circumstances, would allow
acceptable lists to be expanded.*

make it happen automatically that any difficult interaction be logged for study by the system designers, so that the operational difficulties are not invisible to them, even if they don't sit at the system terminal themselves.

provide an "escape to square one" button or simplest possible procedure that always works to untangle the worst possible procedural knot by simply undoing all that went on since the last "square one."

BEING HELPFUL

Not all useful softening can be done with automatic aids. One of the most important principles is that the procedures should be designed to be helpful and to teach better practices to the operator. "Being helpful" means a lot of things, including:

Choose "humble" phrasing of messages so as not to provoke reactions of ill will.

Test message content with people representative of the typical user, and not specialized people like the designers themselves--though they of course must try them too.

Provide at least two alternative message forms to give when the first is not understood, and monitor those forms to find out which ones should be replaced as not helpful.

Protect the system against destruction or damage from wrong procedures. Without such protection, the operator is working under incredible pressure, which will only tend to increase mistakes.

Make common things easy, unless they are potentially dangerous, in which case double check to prevent easy system damage even in "correct" procedures. It is not inconsistent to allow variation in each step and yet require two or more steps to be sure that something irreversible is not done by accident.

Provide an audit trail which can be used as a

last resort to repair damage, and to help the operator learn how to avoid such damage in the future.

LETTING PEOPLE BE SMART

The actual design and programming effort for these tolerances and helpful interactions is a lot less than many imagine. If it really seems too complex a task to handle all variant possibilities in a gentle way, your design is unnecessarily complex. Generalize the error situations into fewer categories and assist the input station operator in helping the computer--by feeding back meaningful information about the situation.

Once again, though, we run into the image of the stupid, poorly-motivated keypunch "girl"--a robot with a boyfriend. For those who object to "letting the keypuncher think," we offer the following observations:

People often behave the way they are expected to behave. Operators treated like robots will act like robots.

Properly humanized procedures will take a lot of data entry out of the isolated keypunch room and bring it to, or closer to, the actual source-- thus eliminating much previous keypunching.

The closer the data entry to the source, the "smarter" the keyers seem to be, for they are more likely to have the information needed to do smart things in response to the dumb things the computer does, or in cooperation with the smart things.

The smarter the keyers are, the less likely they are to tolerate a system that doesn't permit them to think and to make a contribution to the common task.

In sum, the "keypunch girl" as imagined by the backward input designer is an endangered species. And so is the backward designer!

PERFORMANCE ESTIMATES

When input systems tolerate variance, simple computations of performance can give highly misleading estimates. Many designers fear variation because they
can't easily estimate performance. Others make rough,
distorted estimates and use them to dismiss the possibility of permitting variation.

SOURCES OF DISTORTION

By identifying the major sources of distortion,
we can begin to improve estimating. The most common
reasons for difficult estimating are these:

*Source documents are not specifically prepared
for keying convenience.*

*There are several variant forms of source docum-
ent, but the variants are similar enough to be
confusing and are mixed in unpredictable patterns.*

*Keying is not done from source documents at all,
but directly from the transaction source--a telephone call, a factory monitoring station, a portable terminal in the field.*

*The operators are keying as an incidental adjunct
to other responsibilities, not as a full-time
professional commitment.*

The job is a one-time conversion.

For a heart-rending tale of misestimated one-time
conversion involving variant forms not prepared for
computer input, see *Travels in Computerland, or Incom-
patabilities and Interfaces*, by Ben Ross Schneider,
Jr. (1974). Schneider's project involved keying from
a reference work, *The London Stage*. Early in the project, he allowed his programmer to convince him that
variance would not be tolerated. After many travels,
rivalling Gulliver's or Candide's, Schneider--the in-
nocent English professor--was saved by the skill and
dedication of professional data preparation operators
in Hong Kong who proved more effective than any number
of fancy "automatic" input devices--including the

optical scanner for which they were retyping the material.

The Hong Kong operators at least had the advantage of a *serial text*--thanks to some foresight by the programmer. With other types of documents not designed for computer input, the major portion of operator time can be spent *searching* for information rather than actually stroking the keys. Searching may also break the rhythm and induce correlated errors, which is why so many designers opt for a separate form-filling stage--to standardize the sequence. Then they can estimate keying performance rather accurately, but how do they estimate the form-filling?

With a sequence-tolerant input program, estimating search time may actually be easier than estimating the form-filling it eliminates. If *all* source sequences are tolerated, searching is essentially eliminated, and need not be estimated at all. Yet, because the form-filling alternative cannot be estimated, the designer can't really compare methods--and may choose the "traditional" method out of fear of the unknown.

For instance, one of the authors (Gilb) designed a conversion from 60-year-old criminal registers, which existed in 8 different formats. The design was sufficiently variation-tolerant to eliminate all manual encoding, transcription, and "verification" by repetitive keying, but nobody knew how to estimate the alternative methods. Eventually, it was agreed that even with full allowance for programming, design, and additional computer processing, the tolerant design would be *3 to 8 times better* than the best alternative, so the system was used. Other designers might not be so lucky, but these large savings are typical of most tolerant designs when form-filling is eliminated.

ALLOCATING THE COST

Choosing between two designs may not depend solely on cost, but also on *allocation* of cost. Because Schneider's programs and optical scanners wouldn't tolerate much variance, a tremendous burden was placed on a group of dedicated editors (including Schneider

himself) who marked all pages prior to the retyping
demanded by the optical scanners. In comparing the
costs of different alternatives, Schneider counted his
own labor and the labor of all his editors as *free*.

Outside of university research, we seldom find
such large pockets of free labor. Nevertheless, the
labor of one cost center can easily be considered
"free" by another. In estimating two approaches to a
job, one with form-filling, encoding, and repetitive
keying and the other without, the critical factor may
be who will do these jobs. If the data processing department has full responsibility, the savings for
eliminating extra steps will be clear enough. If
these onerous tasks can be sloughed off to someone
else, the more expensive approach may look cheaper--
to the data processing department.

Conversely, design, programming, and computer
processing costs may be higher for the variation-
tolerant job. If they are absorbed into general data
processing "overhead," this approach will look more
favorable to the data processing department, particularly if there is idle programmer or machine time.

In sum, data processing departments are not different from other departments in large bureaucracies.
They will push costs out and pull benefits in whenever
they have the opportunity. It is particularly tempt-
ing to push out those jobs that nobody wants--form-
filling, coding, keypunching, document handling and
control, rekeying, and all the rest. Customer relations often acts as a brake on the pushing out, but
there frequently is a better reason for keeping control of unpleasant tasks, or eliminating them.

When vast numbers of unskilled and uncontrolled
people fill out forms--even when there is no motivation to sabotage or harass--many of the forms will have
to be handled a second time on an exception basis.
These exceptions diminish everyone's productivity, and
must not be overlooked in estimating. When we push
problems out of our cost center, they may return in
a new guise--bigger and uglier. Conversely, happy
customers produce clean input--especially if we're
willing to tolerate their normal variants.

PILOT TESTING

In estimating two approaches to one particular order entry application, the designer computed an average of 21 keystrokes per line item for a fixed-field approach. A sequence-tolerant approach was estimated at 26 strokes for the same messages. The extra strokes were for identification characters, which seemed to imply that the tolerant system would cost 26/21 times the conventional approach.

The estimates were close enough that a pilot test was made. Under the tolerant system, all form-filling was eliminated. This considerable savings had been anticipated, but the observers were surprised to find that even the overall *keying time* was improved under the tolerant system. Moreover, tolerance produced a sizeable reduction in errors:

> *Transcription errors were eliminated, because transcription was eliminated.*
>
> *Using the full source information, rather than a transcribed and abstracted copy, operators were able to make more effective corrections.*
>
> *Stirred by a more varied and responsible task, the operators produced more conscientious work.*

Unfortunately for the designer, there is no way to calculate such savings *in advance*. We must conduct a pilot test. Nevertheless, savings often justify the pilot's cost and delay, so tolerant methods should never be excluded on the basis of raw estimates of keystrokes.

DIRECT ENTRY SYSTEMS

When keying from the transactions themselves, we are even less likely to find keystrokes to be the dominant factor. Over the telephone, for instance, people will invariably give information in a sequence that scrambles the designer's plans, no matter how hard the operator tries to guide the sequence by question-and-answer protocols. With fixed sequences, out-of-order responses require either:

intermediate writing, with possibilities for copying errors

operator memory, with possibilities of misremembering or putting fields out of order

requesting repeated information, with possible customer annoyance, or error

Unfortunately, even when there are specially designed terminals with function keys for each data item type (see Figure 8.2), designers often force a fixed

Sales person	Account number	Division	1	2	3	Cash	Our charge	Void	Reenter
Quantity	Nontaxable	Stock number	4	5	6	Add amount	Other charge	Subtotal	Credit inquiry
			7	8	9				
Paid on account	Employee discount	Other discount	0				Subtract amount	Total	Amount tendered

Figure 8.2 A point-of-sale terminal with function keys for each common data type.

protocol on the operator and customer for programming convenience. When the operators are working full-time at the entry task, they eventually adjust pretty well to the fixed protocols--although they often express job dissatisfaction because of their feeling of subservience to the computer.

When the usage is occasional, the fixed sequence is more annoying, and error-prone. Some direct-entry terminals have the ability to *prompt* each entry--as by illuminating the next identifier key (SALESPERSON, DIVISION, STOCK NUMBER, ... in Figure 8.2) in sequence. Prompting certainly helps the inexperienced operator (though in most designs he has to punch the lighted key anyway). Yet the same prompt may burden the

thought process of some operators--especially those
who are generating the data out of their heads, like
doctors entering patient information.

One design approach allows random order of entry,
using the function keys, if available, for self-identification. After the operator presses the end-of-
transaction key, the system assumes its prompting role
and requests missing mandatory information. This system, like all systems in which variation has been properly designed, is particularly well suited to applications in which there are a large number of optional
or default fields, most of which are not used on any
particular transaction.

In direct entry systems, it's hard to compute total interaction time without actual experience. On
the other hand, exact computations are generally not
critical because the person doing the entry, or providing the information for the entry, is only partly
occupied with the entry task. The keying time will be
a minor component of the total cost, so a precise estimate is not critical.

More important will be estimates of error rate--
and of operator comfort, which will correlate highly
with error rate. Estimates of error frequency, error
type, and operator reaction are best obtained through
a mock-up simulation--especially if we have a human
being behind the console doing the prompting.

PUTTING VARIANCE TO WORK

Variance is a universal human attribute, and human beings are a universal component of the systems we design. Rather than merely putting up with the variance,
perhaps we can put it to work.

SIGNATURES

One type of variance is that *among* individuals.
Rather than seeing this variance as a handicap to be
borne by the system, we can use it to *identify* individuals. When variance is permitted, each operator

will unconsciously adopt an individual *style*--a personal "signature" that the system can recognize, or
that can be presented to humans to recognize. If an
unauthorized person is using the system, his signature
will not be consistent with that of any authorized
person. Properly designed, this kind of security can
be as dependable as fingerprinting and as invisible as
we like, so potential intruders won't even know they
are identifying themselves to the system.

To take a simple example of a signature, suppose
there are 50 possible abbreviations available to the
operators, such as R for REPLY, Y for YES, RA for
READ AGAIN, and REJ for REJECT. If we establish a
50-bit string to record which abbreviations an operat-
or habitually uses, there will be approximately
1,000,000,000,000,000 potential signatures, and few
exact matches will be found. As a session develops,
the signature can be accumulated and matched for consistency against the stored signature of the supposed
operator, to detect an intruder. It would take a most
sophisticated intruder to "forge" the signature of any
other person.

TIMING SIGNATURES

One of the hardest individual patterns to dis-
guise is the pattern of *timing of keystrokes and combinations of keystrokes*. In experiments to study prob-
lem-solving, Weinberg (1965) incidentally discovered
that the timing patterns of responses could be used to
develop a *timing signature* of the individual subject.
Through timing at the 10-100 millisecond level, the
computer could determine that one subject was ambi-
dextrous and that different subjects had different
"homing" positions for the lightpen they were using to
touch the "keys" on the screen.

Not many of today's systems provide such interkey
timing information, but if they did, the information
could easily be used to identify individual operators.
For instance, the sign-on procedure could involve a
"drill," from which the desired patterns could be extracted. Because the variations are on such a high

speed level, they are beneath the conscious level of operator control, and could not be forged by an intruder, no matter how dedicated.

IMPATIENCE

At a slightly slower speed, the system can employ an idea discussed by Gilb (1973), which he called *impatience*. The "impatient" computer takes over automatic correction--even though the probability is rather low--when too long a pause occurs before human correction. As clients subsequently pointed out, this kind of impatience also has security aspects, for a delay could very well indicate an untrained operator trying to break the system.

Such security would be particularly useful if the delay pattern for each authorized operator were recorded and compared on a macroscopic level, much like timing signatures could be compared on a microscopic level.

BLIPS

Over time, the pattern from one individual changes, from

learning in the long run (days)

learning in the short run (hours or minutes)

errors and interruptions in the very short run (on any time scale)

Thus, to use timing patterns for identification, we have to smooth out short run fluctuations and adapt to longer ones. There are well-known techniques for doing these things, some of which we have presented earlier.

Yet these very changes in pattern for one individual can be used in another way, to detect errors. In the same psychological tests, Weinberg (1965) noticed that when a subject made a keying error, a significant delay (a "blip") occured--either just before or just after. This delay was at the level of about

100-300 milliseconds. It was not noticeable to the subject, but had very reliable error-detection proper-ties. The subject know *subconsciously* when he was striking, or had just struck, a wrong response, but only the computer was able to detect the blip. To be sure, subjects often notice quite consciously when a miskeying has been made, but these detected errors are only the tip of the iceberg--part of a continuum with the subconscious errors.

Figure 8.3 shows a hypothetical graph of keystroke timings through a given interval. The times are "nor-malized" to 1.0 for each different stroke by dividing the actual stroke time by the average time for that particular key, or key pair. Thus, with no large dev-iations from pattern, the curve should hover around the 1.0 line.

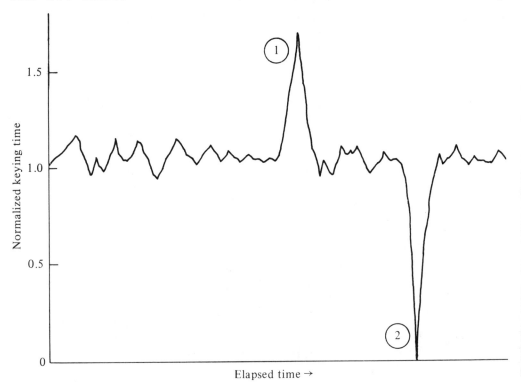

Figure 8.3 Blips in keying time averages may
         indicate errors or poorly designed
         procedures.

At (1), however, there is a sudden upward blip, indicating that the operator broke pattern. This could have been one of several things:

an error about to be made

an error just made, and (subconsciously) realized

a difficult transition in keying, scanning the source, or mental computing

The system can use the error possibility to give the operator a chance to reconsider, as in the following dialogue:

14377 CLAMPS 4"   3 ...

ARE YOU SURE THAT 3 IS THE CORRECT QUANTITY?

NO, 36

The operator forgot to convert the 3 to 3 *dozen*, as suggested to the system by a blip just after the 3.

Blips like (2) in Figure 8.3 represent accidental touching of a key, and would have to be treated differently. Similarly, blips much higher than 2 or 3 times the normal speed are probably *conscious* hesitations, again requiring different action.

Of course, the blip information could be the fault of the system, not the operator. In the above dialogue, the mental computation of dozens into units is likely to be a source of many blips and errors. Appropriate monitoring of blip activity by form and item will enable the designer to spot error-prone areas so that errors can be *prevented*--which is always superior to correction.

ERROR PATTERNS

Not all errors can be prevented, for all people make errors some of the time. But some of the time, they make more errors than other times--another variation pattern we can exploit. Everyone has an occasional bad day, when each error seems to breed more errors. In a system with good error detection properties, it is a simple matter to evaluate if a particular operator is having a disasterous run of luck.

Contrary to certain popular images, most data entry operators are well motivated to do a good job for their pay--so much so that the very motivation can prove harmful. When you're making input errors because of fatigue, preoccupation with a sick child at home, or any number of perfectly good external reasons, trying *harder* only makes things *worse*. When errors and/or error corrections cost money, an hour of input on a bad day can have *negative* net value. It would be wise for the system to suggest a rest period, or a switch to another task, when an operator is experiencing an abnormally high error rate.

Not all variations in error rate are bad. On certain jobs, certain operators do a much more accurate job than others. Generally speaking, these are the jobs they like best. By monitoring error patterns, the computer can suggest work assignments that will lower the error rate, increase the overall productivity, and please the operators--all at the same time. Naturally, human supervision, with override power, would be necessary. Otherwise, people who really didn't like a job would have to make errors just to get switched to another.

People should have some control over the variety of work they do--it's morally right and sound business, besides. Nobody should have to play tricks to get a more satisfying assignment or work environment.

A SERMON

A word or two of caution is in order before we leave the subject of detecting variability and putting it to good use. It would be the easiest thing in the world to turn such information to dehumanizing purposes--particularly as a basis for *suppressing* variability. All we can say in warning is that history shows what happens to tyrants, big and small. It sometimes takes a while, but in the end, tyrants get what they've earned.

Any input designer who is also a student of history will attempt to discover how to convert variance

to reliability, overall system performance, and happi-
ness for the people who touch the system. Any other
approach is an approach to moral and economic bank-
ruptcy.

A SUMMARY OF EXPECTED ATTRIBUTES

The following is a simplified multidimensional view of
the normal attributes which the designer can expect
when specifying some kind of variance toleration. The
designer must calculate or otherwise estimate accurate
attributes for his particular implementation in order
to compare this option against other design alternatives.

PRODUCTIVITY

So many of the "errors" that disrupt the product-
ive flow of information entry work can be attributed
to rigidity on the part of the computer programs acc-
epting the input. An analysis of actual "errors" in
an existing application can give a first order approximation to the increase in productivity which can be
expected once these "errors" are accepted as correct
input--which they would be, but for the designer's
loss of nerve or imagination.

When estimating productivity from increased tolerance, we often have to take into account the elimination of intermediate transcription processes--though
their costs are often distributed to different cost
centers, or out of the organization.

RELIABILITY

Although tolerance seems the opposite of reliability, the actual case is quite different. The inputs
acceptable as "equivalent" to the "true" input can be
controlled so as to screen out nonsense at any level
of desired protection. Reliability may increase because of better operator involvement and acceptance of
the system, and because of elimination of pre-keying
transcription stages. Excessively rigid systems will

invariably stir revolt, even if the revolt is subconscious, and even subconscious revolts produce very real errors entering the system.

PORTABILITY

There is nothing special required to tolerate variance except perhaps larger storage capacity, which may affect downward compatability. New users, of course, will appreciate any tolerance they can get.

IMPLEMENTATION EASE

Programming may be required, but standard routines for common situations can actually make tolerant interaction easier to program than rigid interaction. For coming on the air with a new system, or with new operators, the more tolerant the system is, the fewer bugs and clashes between people and machines.

HARDWARE RESOURCES

Extensive use of humanized input designs can easily result in substantially greater consumption of central processor cycles and secondary storage search time, over programs which effectively place the equivalent work processes on human beings--either before or after the data come to the computer. With normal (Western) costs for people and machines, and with expected cost trends in the future, the automation of this work will tend to be profitable in a reasonably well-designed and "tuned" system. Some direct hardware savings may be made in certain areas, such as

reduced program testing load before operational use

less hardware devoted to training tasks

smaller backup recovery overhead time, from higher quality data causing fewer and less severe system problems

fewer terminals and less transmission time because people complete interactions in much less time

SECURITY

Toleration of variance can make a system easier to penetrate by unauthorized persons. On the other hand, such unauthorized persons will be unable to tell that they are really doing things undetected, because a good system will provide for logging "difficult" interactions in any case. In a properly designed system, the soft interaction will hold an intruder "on the line" long enough for warnings to be given and tracing to be done--in much the same way that "soft" replies can keep an obscene phone caller on the line until the police can intervene.

Specifically protected system areas can be made as "hard" as we like for someone lacking the proper authorization, without making the overall interaction hard at all. We certainly do not need to allow variation in passwords, just because we allow it in the procedure itself.

EXTENDABILITY

Sequence tolerance can make extending messages or lists of messages more difficult, because additional elements vastly increase the number of possible sequences. Extension in other directions can make previously acceptable variations too close to new values, so tolerance systems can be quite growth-sensitive, and must always have monitoring built into them.

In spite of these pitfalls, system extensions seem much easier to design into humanized systems than into conventional systems. The authors' experience in such extensions leads to the conviction that the more humanized the system, the easier the extension. Naturally, careful thought is needed in any extension, but when the system is humanized, it becomes harder to make blunders that aren't noticed by someone as being unnatural.

DESIGN EXERCISES

1. Redesign the system of the first exercise of the
previous Chapter (page 224), seeing if you can make
it more tolerant of normal variations. Discuss and,
if possible, estimate quantitatively, the changes in
system performance that increased tolerance make possible, either positive or negative.

2. The concept of "return to square one" depends on
finding a readily identifiable "square one" that will
be valid for both program and programmer. In some
cases, there are two or more *levels* of "square one,"
as in order entry where the first level is the beginning of all the line items and the second the beginning of the invoice. Level zero might be the beginning of the present line item.

    Taking some input system with which you are fam-
iliar, try to identify the levels of "square one,"
and the procedures (if any) that the operator can use
to get back to them. Identify if possible a simple
key depression that could always be used to return to
square one, and which has the property that N depress-
ions could be used to return to level N of square one.

3. Design a procedure for making "phonetic" equival-
ences of names spoken over the telephone--a procedure
that is alternate to the one described in the chapter.
Your procedure should give rather different keys in
from the same sounds. Estimate how well the two systems would work when used in conjunction. Is there
some checkword that could supplement this performance
in a natural way?

Bibliography

"For the Snark's a peculiar creature that won't
    Be caught in a commonplace way.
Do all that you know, and try all that you don't:
    Not a chance must be wasted today!

"For England expects--I forbear to proceed:
    'Tis a maxim tremendous, but trite:
And you'd best be unpacking the things that you need
    To rig yourselves out for the fight."

                --The Hunting of the Snark, Fit the Fourth

The really good input design, like the Snark, will not
be caught in a commonplace way. When you rig your-
selves out for *that* fight, you'd best unpack a lot
more than you've read here. Fortunately, there *is* a
lot more. This annotated bibliography points to a
wealth of material any input designer can use, though
not all of it has been referenced directly in the book.

Anderson, L. K., R. A. Hendershot, and R. C.
    Schoonmaker
    Self-checking digit concepts.
    Journal of Systems Management, 15, 9 (1974) 36-42

    A comprehensive review of check digit techniques

up to the date of its publication.

Boulding, Kenneth
>*The Image: Knowledge in Life and Society*
>Ann Arbor, Mich.: Univ. of Michigan Press, 1956

>*This long essay or short book sets the stage for thinking about the information systems that are our image of other systems. Required reading for any conscientious systems designer.*

Braverman, Harry
>*Labor and Monopoly Capital: The Degradation of Work in the Twentieth Century*
>New York: Monthly Review Press, 1974

>*How work got organized the way we find it today, showing us things that had been hidden by our lack of historical thinking. Careful but skeptical reading will repay any systems designer manyfold.*

Brown, D. A. H.
>Biquinary decimal error detection codes with one, two and three check digits.
>*Computer Journal*, 17, 3 (August 1974) 201-204

>*Discusses various previous methods of generating check digits with diverse correction and detection properties for decimal numbers. Introduces a set of new methods based on considering each decimal number as a binary part and a quinary part, making a check "digit" for each part, and combining them in a decimal check digit or digits.*

Brown, R. G., and R. F. Meyer
>The fundamental theorem of exponential smoothing.
>*Operations Research*, 9, 5 (Sept-Oct 1961) 673-685

>*The last word on exponential smoothing, extending the method to arbitrary polynomial fitting, with n+1 historical statistics needed to fit an nth order polynomial.*

Campbell, Donald T.
>Systematic error on the part of human links in communication systems.

Information and Control, 1, (1958) 334-369

Human beings demonstrate a pattern in their errors. Campbell classifies many of these patterns and refers to sources of information in the human factors literature.

Carroll, Lewis
  The Hunting of the Snark

Carroll's classic nonsense poem exists today in a variety of editions. One interesting one is The Annotated Snark, *published by Simon and Schuster in 1962 with notes by Martin Gardner. Carroll, being a mathematical logician with a whimsical sense of humor and a devout feeling for the absurd, would have made an excellent systems designer.*

Coaker, Frank W.
  Table-driven input editing for a data-storage
  system.
  Information Storage and Retrieval, 10 (1974) 57-62

The design of an input editing system with the objectives of quick modifiability to handle a variety of formats without reprogramming.

Computing Europe
  Computer sorting bugs US post.
  17 April 1975, 11

Reports the problems of mail sorting in the US Postal Service, with some of the irreverance and smugness that comes from having an ocean between them and the problem.

Cotton, Ira W.
  Remark on stably updating mean and standard
  deviation of data.
  CACM, 18, 8 (August 1975) 458

A parsimonious method of computing running mean and standard deviation.

Dimsdale, B., and G. M. Weinberg
  Programmed error correction in Project Mercury.
  CACM, 4 (Dec 60) 649-651

The first known application of error correction techniques through programming.

Entrex, Inc.
   How to Evaluate and Select a Data Entry System
   168 Middlesex Turnpike, Burlington, Mass. 01803

This undated guidebook was the most useful and systematic of all the materials we received in response to our request. Other firms sending material that would be useful to the designer were (in alphabetical order):

   Ball Computer Products, Inc.
   5601 College Avenue
   Oakland, CA 94618

   Mohawk Data Sciences
   1599 Littleton Road
   Parsippany, NJ 07054

   Raytheon Data Systems
   1415 Boston-Providence Turnpike
   Norwood, Mass. 02062

Fisher, Ronald A.
   The Genetical Theory of Natural Selection
   New York: Dover, 1958 (first published in 1929)

The fundamental work on mathematical genetics-- must reading for designers seriously interested in the adaptive systems of the future.

Florentine, J. J., and A. J. Sammes
   Systems with state re-set.
   The Computer Journal, 18, 2 (1975) 135-139

"State re-set" relates directly to what we have called "resynchronization" in input systems.

Gilb, Tom
   The Codasyl data base task group proposals: a counter-proposal. Simplification and self-optimization.
   IAG Communications, 3/4 (1972)
   (reprinted in *Data Base Management*, Infotech State of the Art Report, 1973, ISBN 8553-9140-5

A proposed overall design strategy for data base management, arguing for a more humanized, adaptive approach than that taken by the Codasyl group.

Reliable EDP Application Design
Lund, Sweden: Studentlitteratur, 1973
ISBN 91-44-06091-2

The source of many new concepts in input design, as well as innovative approaches in the design of reliable EDP systems. Introduces checkwords and adaptive limit checking, elaborates motivational aspects of reliability, and surveys sources of error, to name just a few of the topics.

Laws of unreliability.
Datamation (March 1975) 81-85

A short summary for management (and others) of the deep principles underlying reliable systems.

Data Engineering
Lund, Sweden: Studentlitteratur, 1976

A successor volume to Reliable EDP Application Design, continuing to explore new reliability approaches.

Goldsworthy, A. W.
Generalised input--data editing.
The Australian Computer Journal, 2, 4 (Nov 1970) 166-172

A case study of an input system for applying a variety of conventional editing tests to a number of formats without reprogramming.

Graham, Susan L., and Steven P. Rhodes
Practical syntactic error recovery.
CACM, 18, 11 (Nov 1975) 639-650

Describes a system for recovery from syntactic errors, oriented to programming languages, but interesting for input design in general. Also contains a summary of previous recovery techniques--a useful place to begin a bibliographic search.

Gries, David
Compiler Construction for Digital Computers
New York: John Wiley & Sons, 1971

*An excellent reference for the designer interest-
ed in formal grammars, spelling corrections, and other
compiler-writing techniques that find application in
input systems.*

Gumbel, E. J.
The Statistics of Extremes
New York: Columbia University Press

*The basic, pioneering work on this little-known
branch of statistics--a branch of inordinate interest
to input designers, who work with extremes every day.*

Hoare, C. A. R.
Data reliability.
in *Proceedings of the International Conference on
Reliable Software, SIGPLAN NOTICES,*
10, 6, (June 1975) 528-533

*One of the great original minds in computing
argues strongly why data reliability is so important,
by contrasting data reliability with program reliabil-
ity--the topic of the conference.*

Holmes, W. N.
Identification number design.
The Computer Journal, 18, 2 (Feb 1975) 102-107

*Presents some design approaches to reliability
through the medium of a hypothetical case study of the
design of a set of identification numbers.*

Horn, Robert E.
Information mapping.
Datamation (Jan 1975) 85-88

*Outlines a method for documenting input formats
and procedures, though the examples do not demonstrate
the best possible designs.*

Hunt, Earl B.
Artificial Intelligence

New York: Academic Press, 1975

Most mathematically sophisticated of the artificial intelligence texts referenced here.

Jackson, P. D.
Introduction to Artificial Intelligence
New York: Petrocelli Books, 1974

The least sophisticated and most accessible of the artificial intelligence texts in this bibliography.

Koestler, Arthur
Darkness at Noon
translated by Daphne Hardy
New York: Macmillan, 1941

A gripping "fictional" account of the human drive to communicate in the face of the human drive to persecute--from which our initial quotation was taken, with the kind permission of the copyright holders.

Martin, James
Design of Man-Computer Dialogues
Englewood Cliffs, NJ: Prentice-Hall, 1973

Much broader in coverage than the present volume, including "exotic" input devices as well as output devices and techniques of all types. Much narrower in the sense of its restriction to interactive systems.

Martin, James, and Adrian R. D. Norman
The Computerized Society
Englewood Cliffs, NJ: Prentice-Hall, 1970

Sets the social environment for computing, now and in the future, but unfortunately fails even to mention the data entry personnel who form the bulk of "computerized" employees.

Mayr, Otto
The Origins of Feedback Control
Cambridge, Mass.: MIT Press, 1970

The historical evolution of the concept of feedback in mechanisms, before the computer and Wiener.

Minsky, Marvin
Computation: Finite and Infinite Machines
Englewood Cliffs, NJ: Prentice-Hall, 1967

One of the basic references for automata theory, and a good place for the input designer to begin study of this increasingly relevant discipline.

Minton, G.
Inspection and correction error in data processing.
Journal of the American Statistical Assn.
1969, 1256-1275

A study of duplicate keying which shows the amount of "verified" information remaining as erroneous in later processing stages remains fairly constant at 10%-15%.

Morgan, H. L.
Spelling correction in systems programs.
CACM, 13 (Feb 1970) 90-94

A survey of spelling correction techniques up to 1969, in the field of programming.

Morrison, Philip and Emily, editors
Charles Babbage and His Calculating Engines
New York: Dover, 1961

Charles Babbage was the first computer designer and forsaw most of the problems still facing designers today. A study of his life and frustrations should make the designer realize that not much has changed in the last century as far as acceptance of new ideas.

Mowshowitz, Abbe
The Conquest of Will: Information Processing in Human Affairs
Reading, Mass.: Addison-Wesley, 1976

Another useful view of the role of computers in society, but again ignoring the data entry people.

Naus, Joseph I.
Data Quality Control and Editing

New York: Marcel Dekker, Inc., 1975

*An important reference for input designers inter-
ested in formal approaches to "quality control" of
input--though rather slanted to the interests of the
"scientific" user.*

Nilsson, N. J.
Problem Solving Methods of Artificial Intelligence
New York: McGraw-Hill, 1971

*A text in artificial intelligence which has re-
ceived much support from mathematically trained readers.*

Padgett, M. I.
Tree driven data input and validation.
Computer Journal, 16, 4 (Nov 1973) 315-321

*Describes a "general" technique for the input of
forms to a management information system in which a
large number of different forms would be used. Forms
had to be specified quickly and accurately so that data
could be input without recoding onto intermediate forms.
Padgett's trees permit the description of a wide class
of positional data, including null sections and repeated sections. The system cannot, evidently, be used
to describe identified data.*

Parzen, Emanuel
Modern Probability Theory and Its Applications
New York: John Wiley & Sons, 1960

*A good standard reference to probability theory--
a basic discipline underlying input design. Other
excellent books exist--too many to list them all.*

Schneider, Ben Ross, Jr.
Travels in Computerland
Reading, Mass.: Addison-Wesley, 1974

*A chronicle of the initiation of the uninitiated
to the mysteries of Computerland, particularly to the
mysteries of Keyinputland. To be given as a preventive
to any non-technical person who comes to an input
designer with a problem arising out of work in some
non-computer discipline.*

Shannon, Claude, and Warren Weaver
  The Mathematical Theory of Communication
  Urbana: Univ. of Illinois Press, 1949

  *The first popular presentation of information
theory, which forms the basis of so much of present
mathematical thinking on input design--such as error
correction and detection.*

Slagle, J. R.
  Artificial Intelligence
  New York: McGraw-Hill, 1971

  *Subtitled "the heuristic programming approach,"
this book views artificial intelligence in a manner
that many computer people will find compatible.*

Sonntag, L.
  Designing human-oriented codes.
  Bell Laboratories Record (Feb 1971) 43-49

  *An excellent summary of code design principles
abstracted principally from the less accessible but
more complete* Common Language Coding Guide.

Sterling, Theodor D.
  Guidelines for humanizing computerized informa-
  tion systems.
  CACM, 17, 11 (Nov 1974) 609-613

  *The report of a conference in Canada to "analyze
conditions that may humanize or dehumanize particip-
ants in various computer systems." Some guidelines
apply to data entry situations, though the approach
is rather general because of the broad topic and
short article.*

Taylor, Alan
  The Taylor Report.
  Computerworld 17 Sept 1975 and later issues

  *Demonstrates that self-checking numbers lack
understandability by reporting the sad fate of the
modulus-10 check-digit system used at the Pennsylvania
Bureau of Sales and Use Tax. Taylor's column is one
of the few places showing a consistent concern for*

*input design issues, and serves as something of a
forum for ideas in this area.*

Terkel, Studs
    Working
    New York: Avon Books (paperback), 1975

*A bestselling view of the lot of the worker, this
time in his/her own words, as seen from the salt mines.
Though no remarks of any data entry operator are included, the input designer interested in human beings
will find lots of material directly relevant to this
perplexing business.*

Thompson, D'Arcy
    On Growth and Form (abridged edition)
    John Taylor Bonner, editor
    Cambridge: Cambridge University Press, 1961

*Another essential background book for serious
professional designers. Thompson relates, in aston-
ishing detail, the relationship between the design of
natural systems and the way they evolved and grew.
This book should prove especially thought-provoking to
the designer faced with an existing system of incom-
prehensible design.*

Toffler, Alvin
    Future Shock
    New York: Random House, 1970

*A bestselling view of what the world is coming to,
if present trends continue--an how poorly we are re-
acting to the changes.*

Tomeski, Edward A. and Harold Lazarus
    *People-oriented Computer Systems: The Computer
    in Crisis*
    New York: Van Nostrand-Reinhold, 1975

*Another useful work on the relationship of the
computer to society at large--again failing to mention
the "crisis" in data entry. One has to wonder why
the computer is in crisis--rather than the people who
must cope with the computer in some fashion or the
other.*

Tou, J. T., and R. C. Gonzalez
   Pattern Recognition Principles
   Reading, Mass.: Addison-Wesley, 1974

   A rather more theoretical approach to pattern recognition than Young and Calvert. Offers food for thought on what can be accomplished if adaptive variation based on established patterns is employed.

von Neumann, John
   Theory of Self-Reproducing Automata
   Urbana: University of Illinois Press, 1966

   The original comparison by the "father of computing" of automata to biological systems. The emphasis is on overcoming the failures that machines are heir to by observing how natural systems solve reliability problems.

Weinberg, Gerald M.
   Programmed error correction on a decimal computer.
   CACM, 5, 4 (April 1961) 174-175

   First practical correction scheme using decimal digits.

   Experiments in Problem Solving
   Ann Arbor: University Microfilms, 1965

   Contains the basic observations on timing patterns used to detect subconscious patterns of errors made by operators and to identify different individuals.

   Natural selection as applied to computers and programs.
   General Systems, Vol XV (1970) 145-150

   Application of ideas from natural selection (see R. A. Fisher) to the degredation of reliability in large and not so large computer systems.

   PL/I Programming: A Manual of Style
   New York: McGraw-Hill, 1970

   Contains detailed explanation of a formal grammar that can be used in describing inputs with great variation tolerance.

An Introduction to General Systems Thinking
New York: Wiley Interscience, 1975

*An exploration of the questions an analyst/
designer must ask in the first few minutes of exposure
to a new situation. Covers the Composition Fallacy,
the Axiom of Experience, the Strong Connection Law,
and many other general laws of systems analysis.*

Weinberg, Gerald M., and George L. Gressett
An experiment in automatic verification of
programs.
CACM, 7, 10 (Oct 1963) 610-613

*A methodology for simulating complex error detec-
tion and correction systems using the actual routines
with simulated errors.*

Weinberg, Gerald M., Norie Yasukawa, and Robert Marcus
Structured Programming in PL/C: An Abecedarian
New York: John Wiley & Sons, 1973

*Contains examples of several programming tech-
niques for input discussed in this book, such as
finite-state machines and sound coding for spelling
correction.*

Wiener, Norbert
*The Human Use of Human Beings: Cybernetics and
Society, 2nd edition*
Garden City, NY: Doubleday, 1956

*The first loud cry of a technologist about what
he hath wrought--loud, but generally ignored, as seems
to be the fate of such cries up until now.*

Wilcox, Tom
Introduction to Compiler Construction
Cambridge, Mass.: Winthrop, in press

*A rather more up-to-date reference on compiler
techniques (compared with Gries) that may prove useful
to input designers.*

Young, Tzay Y., and Thomas W. Calvert
Classification, Estimation, and Pattern

Recognition
New York: American Elsevier, 1974

A textbook, less theoretical than Tou and Gonzalez, covering theory and applications of pattern recognition, with suggestions for allowing patterns to help our systems adapt.

Zipf, G. K.
Human Behavior and the Principle of Least Effort
Cambridge, Mass.: Addison-Wesley, 1949

Zipf's Law indicates that the most commonly used words and grammatical forms in a language come, over time, to be the shortest. Zipf is another of the great original thinkers (along with such as Thompson, Fisher, Shannon, Wiener, Babbage, and von Neumann) whose thought permeates, or should permeate, the design of technology.

Index